# Comfortable Crochet Socks

Published by Stackpole Books

An imprint of The Rowman & Littlefield Publishing Group, Inc.

4501 Forbes Blvd., Ste. 200

Lanham, MD 20706

www.stackpolebooks.com

Distributed by NATIONAL BOOK NETWORK

800-462-6420

© 2019 Kosmos Uitgevers and Sascha Blase-Van Wagtendonk, Utrecht/Antwerpen,
part of VBK | media
Patterns: Sascha Blase-Van Wagtendonk, with a great deal of thanks to Ans Baart
Graphic Design: Sigrid Bliekendaal
Handlettering font: Marjet Verhoef
Illustrations: Sigrid Bliekendaal & Marjet Verhoef
Photography: Esther Befort, Sterstijl

British Library Cataloguing-in-Publication Information available

**Library of Congress Cataloging-in-Publication Data**

Names: Blase-van Wagtendonk, Sascha, author. | Befort, Esther, photographer (expression) | Blase-Van
    Wagtendonk, Sascha. Sokken haken à la Sascha.

Title: Comfortable crochet socks / Sascha Blase-Van Wagtendonk ; photography, Esther Befort, Sterstijl.

Other titles: Sokken haken à la Sascha. English

Description: First edition. | Guilford, Connecticut : Stackpole Books, [2021] | Summary: "Sascha Blase-Van
    Wagtendonk has discovered the secrets to perfect-fitting and comfortable crochet socks, and has designed
    ten patterns for the ultimate in style and comfort. All patterns are presented in a range of sizes from babies
    and toddlers through adult, and for both men and women, so every foot can be warm and happy"— Provided
    by publisher.

Identifiers: LCCN 2020056320 (print) | LCCN 2020056321 (ebook) | ISBN 9780811739986 (paperback) | ISBN
    9780811769846 (epub)

Subjects: LCSH: Crocheting—Patterns. | Socks.

Classification: LCC TT825 .B55513 2021 (print) | LCC TT825 (ebook) | DDC 746.43/4041—dc23

LC record available at https://lccn.loc.gov/2020056320

LC ebook record available at https://lccn.loc.gov/2020056321

∞™ The paper used in this publication meets the minimum requirements of American National Standard for
Information Sciences—Permanence of Paper for Printed Library Materials, ANSI/NISO Z39.48-1992.

First Edition

# Comfortable Crochet Socks

## PERFECT-FIT PATTERNS FOR HAPPY FEET

Sascha Blase-Van Wagtendonk

Stackpole
Books
GUILFORD, CONNECTICUT

# FOREWORD

This book started with a a beautiful pair of knitted socks,
which I received as a maternity gift last year from my friend
Ans. I immediately thought that it had to be possible to adapt
that method into a crocheted version. I had crocheted socks
before, but they were always very stiff and not nearly as
beautiful as her knitted ones...

The idea kept running through my mind and I started to design.
I tried many different ways of crocheting socks until I
designed the perfect pattern—a delicious elastic sock that
fit well and was also beautiful. From there I thought of many
different variations, shared with you in this book.

They are so much fun to make and lovely to wear! I am very
proud of this book and very much hope you like it and have as
much fun crocheting socks as I do!

Love, Sascha

# CONTENTS

foreword
p.07

## Chapter 1
## MATERIALS
p.10

## Chapter 2
## SOCK YARN
p.12

## Chapter 3
## SIZES AND
## PROPORTIONS
p.14

## Chapter 4
## CROCHET STITCHES
p.18

## Chapter 5
## PATTERNS
p.22 — 121

## Chapter 6
## TIPS AND EXTRAS
p.122

acknowledgments
p.124

sponsors
p.125

about the author
p.127

patterns
CAT'S-EYE SOCKS
p.24

ARMADILLO SOCKS
p.34

BUTTERFLY SOCKS
p.42

LOCOMOTIVE SOCKS
p.52

COFFEE BEAN SOCKS
p.62

LITTLE BEAR SOCKS
p.72

VEILTAIL SOCKS
p.82

CABLE CAR SOCKS
p.92

CRANE SOCKS
p.102

HONEYCOMB SOCKS
p.110

# CONTENTS

24

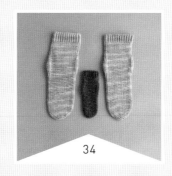
34

42

52

62

72

82

92

102

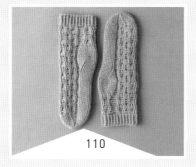
110

# Chapter 1

# materials

—— —— —— —— —— ——

**Crochet Hooks**
Many crocheters still use the thin metal hooks from Grandmother's time, but now there are a lot of beautiful and practical options! There are many ergonomic designs that feel a lot more pleasant in your hands. Wooden crochet hooks come in many variations and are definitely worth a try.

You will likely find either metal or wood more pleasant to work with; few crocheters use both. Wood is a lot warmer in the hand and has a little more grip on the yarn, where a metal or plastic hook is a lot smoother and slides easily through the yarn. The most special crochet hooks are handmade, as shown in the picture! Allan Marshall of Bowltech Crochet Hooks makes the chic wooden ergonomic crochet hooks, and Jessica Kouwenhoven-Schild from StudioForestFriends makes the beautiful rustic hand-cut twig crochet hooks.

## Stitch Markers

Stitch markers mark stitches where, for example, a stitch must be increased or decreased, but they also can indicate your end or starting point. There are several types of plastic and metal markers on the market, but a paper clip or safety pin also works fine.

## Yarn Needle

You will need a thick needle with a large eye for finishing the socks.

## Scissors

Use a fine, sharp pair of scissors to cut yarn.

## Measuring Tape

Measuring is indispensable for matching the stitching gauge, and it's helpful for sizing.

## Project Bag

A small tote will keep your socks neat and clean and easily portable—because you can crochet socks anywhere!

# sock yarn

ooooooooooooooooooooooooooooooooooooooooooo

You can find sock yarn in many types and varieties. All socks in this book are crocheted with the most common thickness, 4-ply sock yarn for hook sizes US B-1 to E-4 (2.5 to 3.5 mm). You will almost always find this thickness on skeins of 3.5 oz./459 yd. (100 g./420 m) or 1.7 oz./230 yd. (50 g./210 m). Here is a small overview of the differences in yarn attributes.

## Origin

The most common sock yarns are made from sheep wool. This means that the wool has been sheared directly from a live sheep. This material has the perfect properties for socks! It is very strong and durable, but it is also moisture-absorbent and breathable. Other animal fibers used are merino wool from the merino sheep, alpaca wool, or even cashmere for softer, more luxurious socks. Cotton yarn is also available. Cotton has a completely different effect than wool. It wears and crochets very pleasantly, but to make it stretchy, elastic is added to the cotton yarn, which gives it a different feel when you crochet with it. Cotton will give your stitches very nice definition, but crocheting with cotton takes some getting used to.

## Appearance

Skeins of sock yarn are often so beautiful that this is reason enough for an enthusiast to buy them! Of course you can make nice color patterns with single-color yarns, but you can also buy skeins in which the color pattern is already incorporated. For example, you will find yarns with short repeating runs of color that are especially fun with simple patterns such as the Cat's-eye or Armadillo socks in this book. Long gradients are suitable for more intricate patterns, such as the Veiltail or Coffee Bean socks. I also love heathered and tweed yarns. These two variants seem plainer, but they make your pattern take center stage and give it just a little extra depth!

# Chapter 3

## sizes and proportions

| | | | | | | | | | | | | | | | | | | | | | | | | | | | | | | | | | | | | | | | | | | | |

### SIZE

It is best to choose a sock size based on the size of the foot. If you do not know the size or have measurements, you can also choose by age or estimated size, but this can be a bit of a risk. The socks are made to be spacious. If you are in doubt between two sizes, choose the smaller. There is a pattern for every size, but not every pattern includes all sizes; you can find the available sizes in each pattern.

| | Foot Length Max | Foot Circumference Max |
|---|---|---|
| 0–6 months | 4.7 in./12 cm | 3.9 in./10 cm |
| 12–24 months | 5.9 in./15 cm | 4.9 in./12.5 cm |
| 3–5 years | 7.1 in./18 cm | 5.9 in./15 cm |
| 6–10 years | 8.3 in./21 cm | 6.9 in./17.5 cm |
| Small | 9.4 in./24 cm | 7.9 in./20 cm |
| Medium | 10.6 in./27 cm | 8.9 in./22.5 cm |
| Large | 11.8 in./30 cm | 9.8 in./25 cm |

## GAUGE

To be sure your socks turn out the size you want, check your gauge. To do this, make a small test piece (or at least check the gauge as you crochet); measure the stitches and compare them to this gauge:

5 sts wide and 4 rnds high = 0.7 in./2 cm square

If your ratio doesn't match, try a different size crochet hook. If you have more stitches than this ratio, try a larger crochet hook (US size 7/4.5 mm); if you have fewer stitches, try a smaller crochet hook (US size E-4/3.5 mm).

|  | Width (measured flat) | Length (measured flat from the tip of the toe) |
|---|---|---|
| 0–6 months | At round 8: ± between 2–2.4 in./ 5–6 cm | At round 8: ± 1.6 in./4 cm |
| 12–24 months | At round 12: ± between 2.4–2.8 in./ 6–7 cm | At round 12: ± 2.4 in./6 cm |
| 3–5 years | At round 16: ± between 2.8–3.2 in./ 7–8 cm | At round 16: ± 3.2 in./8 cm |
| 6–10 years | At round 20: ± between 3.2–3.5 in./ 8–9 cm | At round 20: ± 3.9 in./10 cm |
| Small | At round 24: ± between 3.5–3.9 in./ 9–10 cm | At round 24: ± 4.7 in./12 cm |
| Medium | At round 28: ± between 3.9–4.3 in./ 10–11 cm | At round 28: ± 5.5 in./14 cm |
| Large | At round 32: ± between 4.3–4.7 in./ 11–12 cm | At round 32: ± 6.3 in./16 cm |

# Chapter 4

## crochet stitches

---

### MAGIC LOOP

Make a circle of the yarn; the working yarn should be over the yarn end. Insert your crochet hook into the ring and wrap the working yarn from back to front so that you have a yarn over on your crochet hook. Pull the yarn over through the ring, yarn over again, and hook one chain stitch. Then crochet the number of stitches into the ring as the pattern states, working around both the yarn of the ring and the loose end. Once you have the desired number of stitches, pull the loose end tight to close the ring. Continue working according to the pattern.

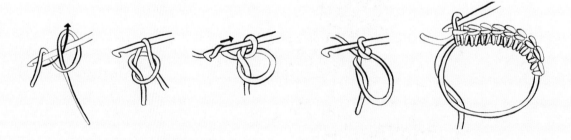

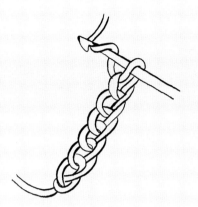

## CHAIN

In the illustration, there is a setup chain already on the crochet hook; otherwise, begin with a slipknot on your hook. Insert the crochet hook under the working yarn so that you put a wrap, or yarn over, on your hook, and then pull the yarn through the loop on your hook. You have a single crochet.

## SLIP STITCH

Insert the crochet hook into the stitch from front to back, yarn over with the working yarn, then pull the yarn through the two loops on your hook. You have worked a slip stitch.

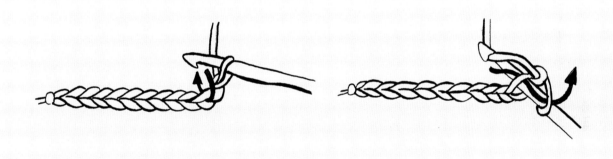

## SINGLE CROCHET

Insert the crochet hook from front to back, yarn over with the working yarn, then pull the yarn through the stitch. Yarn over again and pull the working yarn through the two loops on your hook. You have made a single crochet.

## HALF DOUBLE CROCHET

Yarn over your crochet hook from back to front and insert the hook into the stitch from front to back. Yarn over and pull the yarn through the stitch. You have three loops on your hook. Yarn over again and pull the yarn through all three loops. You have made a half double crochet.

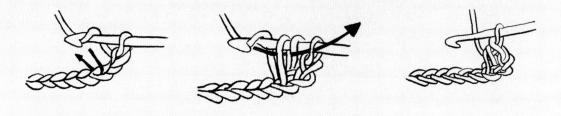

## DOUBLE CROCHET

Yarn over your crochet hook from back to front and insert the hook into the stitch from front to back. Yarn over and pull the yarn through the stitch. You have three loops on your hook. Yarn over again and pull the yarn through two of the loops on your hook. Yarn over again and pull the yarn through the last two loops on your hook. You have worked a double crochet.

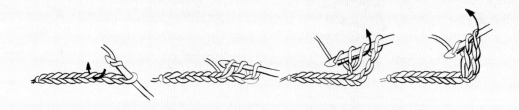

## TREBLE CROCHET

Wrap yarn over your crochet hook twice from back to front so you have two yarn overs on your hook. Insert the hook into the stitch from front to back, yarn over, and pull the yarn through the stitch, * yarn over again, pull it through the first two loops on your hook *, repeat from * to * two more times. You have worked a treble crochet.

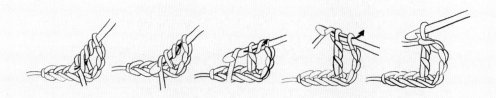

## POST STITCHES

Post stitches are just like normal stitches, but instead of your hook going into the top of the stitch, you work the hook around the leg of the stitch.

### Front Post Double Crochet

For a front post double crochet, yarn over and insert the hook from front to back behind the stitch and back to the front again; then work the double crochet as usual.

### Back Post Double Crochet

Work just like a normal double crochet stitch, but instead of inserting the hook into the top of the stich, work it around the leg of the stitch from back to front and back behind again.

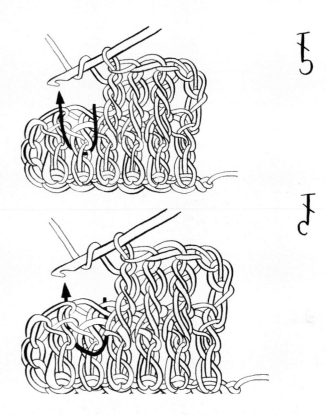

### Front Post Half Double Crochet

Work just like a normal half double crochet, but insert the hook around the stitch from front to back and then to the front again.

### Back Post Half Double Crochet

Work just like a normal half double crochet, but insert the hook around the stitch from back to front and then to the back again.

### Front Post Treble Crochet

Work just like a normal treble crochet, but insert the hook around the stitch from front to back and then to the front again.

### Back Post Treble Crochet

Work just like a normal treble crochet, but insert the hook around the stitch from front to back and then to the front again.

# Chapter 5

## patterns

————— —— ——— —— —— —— — ———

# cat's-eye

THE CAT'S-EYE SOCK IS THE BASIC PATTERN OF THIS BOOK.
IT IS A DELICIOUS PATTERN TO START WITH AND WORKS
PERFECTLY WITH SOCK YARN OF ANY COLOR.

For help in choosing the right size, see page 15.
For help in choosing the right hook size and checking gauge, see page 16.

## MATERIALS

**Yarn**
**Blue socks:**   Durable Soqs; #1 super fine weight (75% wool,
25% polyamide; 230 yd./210 m per 1.76 oz./
50 g.); color #289

**Coral socks:**   Lang Yarn Jawoll Twin, #1 super fine weight
(75% wool, 25% nylon/polyamide; 230 yd./210 m;
1.76 oz./50 g); color #504

**Hook**
US size G-6 (4 mm)

**Gauge**
5 fpdc wide and 4 rnds high = 0.7 in./2 cm

**Estimated total yarn required**
0–6 months: 230 yd./210 m; 12–24 months: 230 yd./210 m; 3–5
years: 460 yd./420 m; 6–10 years: 460 yd./420 m; Small: 460
yd./420 m; Medium: 689 yd./630 m; Large: 689 yd./630 m

## ABBREVIATIONS

| | | |
|---|---|---|
| ◯ | **ch** | chain |
| ┬ | **dc** | double crochet |
| ⌠ | **fpdc** | front post double crochet |
| ⌡ | **bpdc** | back post double crochet |
| ⬤ | **sl st** | slip stitch |
| ⋀ | **fpdc2tog** | front post double crochet 2 together (1 stitch decreased) |
| ⋁ | **2 fpdc in the next stitch** | 2 fpdc in the same stitch (1 stitch increased) |

Rnd 1:   Start with a magic loop, ch2 (first ch2 doesn't count as first dc throughout), 6dc in the loop, sl st in first dc. (6)

Rnd 2:   Ch2, 2fpdc in each st around, sl st in first fpdc. (12)

Rnd 3:   Ch2, *fpdc1, 2fpdc in next stitch*, repeat * to * 2 more times, hdc1, 2fpdc in next stitch, repeat * to * 2 more times, sl st in first fpdc. (18)

Rnd 4:   Ch2, *fpdc2, 2fpdc in next stitch*, repeat * to * 2 more times, hdc1, fpdc1, 2fpdc in next stitch, repeat * to * 2 more times, sl st in first fpdc. (24)

Rnds 5-12: Ch2, fpdc12, hdc1, fpdc11, sl st in first fpdc. (24)

Rnd 13:  Ch2, 2fpdc in next stitch, fpdc10, 2fpdc in next stitch, hdc1, fpdc11, sl st in first fpdc. (26)

Rnd 14:  Ch2, fpdc1, 2fpdc in next stitch, fpdc10, 2fpdc in next stitch, fpdc1, hdc1, fpdc11, sl st in first fpdc. (28)

Rnd 15:  Ch2, fpdc2, 2fpdc in next stitch, fpdc10, 2fpdc in next stitch, fpdc2, hdc1, fpdc11, sl st in first fpdc. (30)

Rnd 16:  Ch2, fpdc2, fpdc2tog, fpdc10, fpdc2tog, fpdc2, hdc1, fpdc11, sl st in first fpdc. (28)

Rnd 17:  Ch2, fpdc1, fpdc2tog, fpdc10, fpdc2tog, fpdc1, hdc1, fpdc11, sl st in first fpdc. (26)

Rnd 18:  Ch2, fpdc2tog, fpdc10, fpdc2tog, hdc1, fpdc11, sl st in first fpdc. (24)

Rnds 19-21: Ch2, fpdc12, hdc1, fpdc11, sl st in first fpdc. (24)

Rnds 22-24: Ch2, *fpdc1, bpdc1*, repeat * to * around, sl st in first fpdc. (24)

Fasten off and weave in ends.

Rnd 1:   Start with a magic loop, ch2 (first ch2 doesn't count as first dc throughout), 6dc in the loop, sl st in first dc. (6)

Rnd 2:   Ch2, 2fpdc in each stitch around, sl st in first fpdc. (12)

Rnd 3:   Ch2, *fpdc1, 2fpdc in next stitch*, repeat * to * 2 more times, hdc1, 2fpdc in next stitch, repeat * to * 2 more times, sl st in first fpdc. (18)

Rnd 4:   Ch2, *fpdc2, 2fpdc in next stitch*, repeat * to * 2 more times, hdc1, fpdc1, 2fpdc in next stitch, repeat * to * 2 more times, sl st in first fpdc. (24)

Rnd 5:   Ch2, *fpdc3, 2fpdc in next stitch*, repeat * to * 2 more times, hdc1, fpdc2, 2fpdc in next stitch, repeat * to * 2 more times, sl st in first fpdc. (30)

Rnds 6-17: Ch2, fpdc15, hdc1, fpdc14, sl st in first fpdc. (30)

Rnd 18:  Ch2, 2fpdc in next stitch, fpdc13, 2fpdc in next stitch, hdc1, fpdc14, sl st in first fpdc. (32)

Rnd 19:  Ch2, fpdc1, 2fpdc in next stitch, fpdc13, 2fpdc in next stitch, fpdc1, hdc1, fpdc14, sl st in first fpdc. (34)

Rnd 20:  Ch2, fpdc2, 2fpdc in next stitch, fpdc13, 2fpdc in next stitch, fpdc2, hdc1, fpdc14, sl st in first fpdc. (36)

Rnd 21:  Ch2, fpdc3, 2fpdc in next stitch, fpdc13, 2fpdc in next stitch, fpdc3, hdc1, fpdc14, sl st in first fpdc. (38)

Rnd 22:  Ch2, fpdc3, fpdc2tog, fpdc13, fpdc2tog, fpdc3, hdc1, fpdc14, sl st in first fpdc. (36)

Rnd 23:  Ch2, fpdc2, fpdc2tog, fpdc13, fpdc2tog, fpdc2, hdc1, fpdc14, sl st in first fpdc. (34)

Rnd 24:  Ch2, fpdc1, fpdc2tog, fpdc13, fpdc2tog, fpdc1, hdc1, fpdc14, sl st in first fpdc. (32)

Rnd 25:  Ch2, fpdc2tog, fpdc13, fpdc2tog, hdc1, fpdc14, sl st in first fpdc. (30)

Rnds 26-28: Ch2, fpdc15, hdc1, fpdc14, sl st in first fpdc. (30)

Rnds 29-31: Ch2, *fpdc1, bpdc1*, repeat * to * around, sl st in first fpdc. (30)

Fasten off and weave in ends.

Rnd 1:   Start with a magic loop, ch2 (first ch2 doesn't count as first dc throughout), 6dc in the loop, sl st in first dc. (6)

**Rnd 2:** Ch2, 2fpdc in each stitch around, sl st in first fpdc. (12)

**Rnd 3:** Ch2, *fpdc1, 2fpdc in next stitch*, repeat * to * 2 more times, hdc1, 2fpdc in next stitch, repeat * to * 2 more times, sl st in first fpdc. (18)

**Rnd 4:** Ch2, *fpdc2, 2fpdc in next stitch*, repeat * to * 2 more times, hdc1, fpdc1, 2fpdc in next stitch, repeat * to * 2 more times, sl st in first fpdc. (24)

**Rnd 5:** Ch2, *fpdc3, 2fpdc in next stitch*, repeat * to * 2 more times, hdc1, fpdc2, 2fpdc in next stitch, repeat * to * 2 more times, sl st in first fpdc. (30)

**Rnd 6:** Ch2, *fpdc4, 2fpdc in next stitch*, repeat * to * 2 more times, hdc1, fpdc3, 2fpdc in next stitch, repeat * to * 2 more times, sl st in first fpdc. (36)

**Rnds 7-22:** Ch2, fpdc18, hdc1, fpdc17, sl st in first fpdc. (36)

**Rnd 23:** Ch2, 2fpdc in next stitch, fpdc16, 2fpdc in next stitch, hdc1, fpdc17, sl st in first fpdc. (38)

**Rnd 24:** Ch2, fpdc1, 2fpdc in next stitch, fpdc16, 2fpdc in next stitch, fpdc1, hdc1, fpdc17, sl st in first fpdc. (40)

**Rnd 25:** Ch2, fpdc2, 2fpdc in next stitch, fpdc16, 2fpdc in next stitch, fpdc2, hdc1, fpdc17, sl st in first fpdc. (42)

**Rnd 26:** Ch2, fpdc3, 2fpdc in next stitch, fpdc16, 2fpdc in next stitch, fpdc3, hdc1, fpdc17, sl st in first fpdc. (44)

**Rnd 27:** Ch2, fpdc4, 2fpdc in next stitch, fpdc16, 2fpdc in next stitch, fpdc4, hdc1, fpdc17, sl st in first fpdc. (46)

**Rnd 28:** Ch2, fpdc4, fpdc2tog, fpdc16, fpdc2tog, fpdc4, hdc1, fpdc17, sl st in first fpdc. (44)

**Rnd 29:** Ch2, fpdc3, fpdc2tog, fpdc16, fpdc2tog, fpdc3, hdc1, fpdc17, sl st in first fpdc. (42)

**Rnd 30:** Ch2, fpdc2, fpdc2tog, fpdc16, fpdc2tog, fpdc2, hdc1, fpdc17, sl st in first fpdc. (40)

**Rnd 31:** Ch2, fpdc1, fpdc2tog, fpdc16, fpdc2tog, fpdc1, hdc1, fpdc17, sl st in first fpdc. (38)

**Rnd 32:** Ch2, fpdc2tog, fpdc16, fpdc2tog, hdc1, fpdc17, sl st in first fpdc. (36)

**Rnds 33-37:** Ch2, fpdc18, hdc1, fpdc17, sl st in first fpdc. (36)

**Rnds 38-41:** Ch2, *fpdc1, bpdc1*, repeat * to * around, sl st in first fpdc. (36)
Fasten off and weave in ends.


**SIZE: 6-10 YEARS**

**Rnd 1:** Start with a magic loop, ch2 (first ch2 doesn't count as first dc throughout), 6dc in the loop, sl st in first dc. (6)

**Rnd 2:** Ch2, 2fpdc in each stitch around, sl st in first fpdc. (12)

**Rnd 3:** Ch2, *fpdc1, 2fpdc in next stitch*, repeat * to * 2 more times, hdc1, 2fpdc in next stitch, repeat * to * 2 more times, sl st in first fpdc. (18)

**Rnd 4:** Ch2, *fpdc2, 2fpdc in next stitch*, repeat * to * 2 more times, hdc1, fpdc1, 2fpdc in next stitch, repeat * to * 2 more times, sl st in first fpdc. (24)

**Rnd 5:** Ch2, *fpdc3, 2fpdc in next stitch*, repeat * to * 2 more times, hdc1, fpdc2, 2fpdc in next stitch, repeat * to * 2 more times, sl st in first fpdc. (30)

**Rnd 6:** Ch2, *fpdc4, 2fpdc in next stitch*, repeat * to * 2 more times, hdc1, fpdc3, 2fpdc in next stitch, repeat * to * 2 more times, sl st in first fpdc. (36)

**Rnd 7:** Ch2, *fpdc5, 2fpdc in next stitch*, repeat * to * 2 more times, hdc1, fpdc4, 2fpdc in next stitch, repeat * to * 2 more times, sl st in first fpdc. (42)

**Rnds 8-27:** Ch2, fpdc21, hdc1, fpdc20, sl st in first fpdc. (42)

**Rnd 28:** Ch2, 2fpdc in next stitch, fpdc19, 2fpdc in next stitch, hdc1, fpdc20, sl st in first fpdc. (44)

**Rnd 29:** Ch2, fpdc1, 2fpdc in next stitch, fpdc19, 2fpdc in next stitch, fpdc1, hdc1, fpdc20, sl st in first fpdc. (46)

**Rnd 30:** Ch2, fpdc2, 2fpdc in next stitch, fpdc19, 2fpdc in next stitch, fpdc2, hdc1, fpdc20, sl st in first fpdc. (48)

**Rnd 31:** Ch2, fpdc3, 2fpdc in next stitch, fpdc19, 2fpdc in next stitch, fpdc3, hdc1, fpdc20, sl st in first fpdc. (50)

**Rnd 32:** Ch2, fpdc4, 2fpdc in next stitch, fpdc19, 2fpdc in next stitch, fpdc4, hdc1, fpdc20, sl st in first fpdc. (52)

**Rnd 33:** Ch2, fpdc5, 2fpdc in next stitch, fpdc19, 2fpdc in next stitch, fpdc5, hdc1, fpdc20, sl st in first fpdc. (54)

**Rnd 34:** Ch2, fpdc5, fpdc2tog, fpdc19, fpdc2tog, fpdc5, hdc1, fpdc20, sl st in first fpdc. (52)

**Rnd 35:** Ch2, fpdc4, fpdc2tog, fpdc19, fpdc2tog, fpdc4, hdc1, fpdc20, sl st in first fpdc. (50)

**Rnd 36:** Ch2, fpdc3, fpdc2tog, fpdc19, fpdc2tog, fpdc3, hdc1, fpdc20, sl st in first fpdc. (48)

**Rnd 37:** Ch2, fpdc2, fpdc2tog, fpdc19, fpdc2tog, fpdc2, hdc1, fpdc20, sl st in first fpdc. (46)

**Rnd 38:** Ch2, fpdc1, fpdc2tog, fpdc19, fpdc2tog, fpdc1, hdc1, fpdc20, sl st in first fpdc. (44)

**Rnd 39:** Ch2, fpdc2tog, fpdc19, fpdc2tog, hdc1, fpdc20, sl st in first fpdc. (42)

**Rnds 40–45:** Ch2, fpdc21, hdc1, fpdc20, sl st in first fpdc. (42)

**Rnds 46–51:** Ch2, *fpdc1, bpdc1*, repeat * to * around, sl st in first fpdc. (42)

Fasten off and weave in ends.

## SIZE: SMALL

**Rnd 1:** Start with a magic loop, ch2 (first ch2 doesn't count as first dc throughout), 6dc in the loop, sl st in first dc. (6)

**Rnd 2:** Ch2, 2fpdc in each stitch around, sl st in first fpdc. (12)

**Rnd 3:** Ch2, *fpdc1, 2fpdc in next stitch*, repeat * to * 2 more times, hdc1, 2fpdc in next stitch, repeat * to * 2 more times, sl st in first fpdc. (18)

**Rnd 4:** Ch2, *fpdc2, 2fpdc in next stitch*, repeat * to * 2 more times, hdc1, fpdc1, 2fpdc in next stitch, repeat * to * 2 more times, sl st in first fpdc. (24)

**Rnd 5:** Ch2, *fpdc3, 2fpdc in next stitch*, repeat * to * 2 more times, hdc1, fpdc2, 2fpdc in next stitch, repeat * to * 2 more times, sl st in first fpdc. (30)

**Rnd 6:** Ch2, *fpdc4, 2fpdc in next stitch*, repeat * to * 2 more times, hdc1, fpdc3, 2fpdc in next stitch, repeat * to * 2 more times, sl st in first fpdc. (36)

**Rnd 7:** Ch2, *fpdc5, 2fpdc in next stitch*, repeat * to * 2 more times, hdc1, fpdc4, 2fpdc in next stitch, repeat * to * 2 more times, sl st in first fpdc. (42)

**Rnd 8:** Ch2, *fpdc6, 2fpdc in next stitch*, repeat * to * 2 more times, hdc1, fpdc5, 2fpdc in next stitch, repeat * to * 2 more times, sl st in first fpdc. (48)

**Rnds 9–32:** Ch2, fpdc24, hdc1, fpdc23, sl st in first fpdc. (48)

**Rnd 33:** Ch2, 2fpdc in next stitch, fpdc22, 2fpdc in next stitch, hdc1, fpdc23, sl st in first fpdc. (50)

**Rnd 34:** Ch2, fpdc1, 2fpdc in next stitch, fpdc22, 2fpdc in next stitch, fpdc1, hdc1, fpdc23, sl st in first fpdc. (52)

**Rnd 35:** Ch2, fpdc2, 2fpdc in next stitch, fpdc22, 2fpdc in next stitch, fpdc2, hdc1, fpdc23, sl st in first fpdc. (54)

**Rnd 36:** Ch2, fpdc3, 2fpdc in next stitch, fpdc22, 2fpdc in next stitch, fpdc3, hdc1, fpdc23, sl st in first fpdc. (56)

**Rnd 37:** Ch2, fpdc4, 2fpdc in next stitch, fpdc22, 2fpdc in next stitch, fpdc4, hdc1, fpdc23, sl st in first fpdc. (58)

**Rnd 38:** Ch2, fpdc5, 2fpdc in next stitch, fpdc22, 2fpdc in next stitch, fpdc5, hdc1, fpdc23, sl st in first fpdc. (60)

**Rnd 39:** Ch2, fpdc6, 2fpdc in next stitch, fpdc22, 2fpdc in next stitch, fpdc6, hdc1, fpdc23, sl st in first fpdc. (62)

**Rnd 40:** Ch2, fpdc6, fpdc2tog, fpdc22, fpdc2tog, fpdc6, hdc1, fpdc23, sl st in first fpdc. (60)

**Rnd 41:** Ch2, fpdc5, fpdc2tog, fpdc22, fpdc2tog, fpdc5, hdc1, fpdc23, sl st in first fpdc. (58)

**Rnd 42:** Ch2, fpdc4, fpdc2tog, fpdc22, fpdc2tog, fpdc4, hdc1, fpdc23, sl st in first fpdc. (56)

**Rnd 43:** Ch2, fpdc3, fpdc2tog, fpdc22, fpdc2tog, fpdc3, hdc1, fpdc23, sl st in first fpdc. (54)

**Rnd 44:** Ch2, fpdc2, fpdc2tog, fpdc22, fpdc2tog, fpdc2, hdc1, fpdc23, sl st in first fpdc. (52)

**Rnd 45:** Ch2, fpdc1, fpdc2tog, fpdc22, fpdc2tog, fpdc1, hdc1, fpdc23, sl st in first fpdc. (50)

**Rnd 46:** Ch2, fpdc2tog, fpdc22, fpdc2tog, hdc1, fpdc23, sl st in first fpdc. (48)

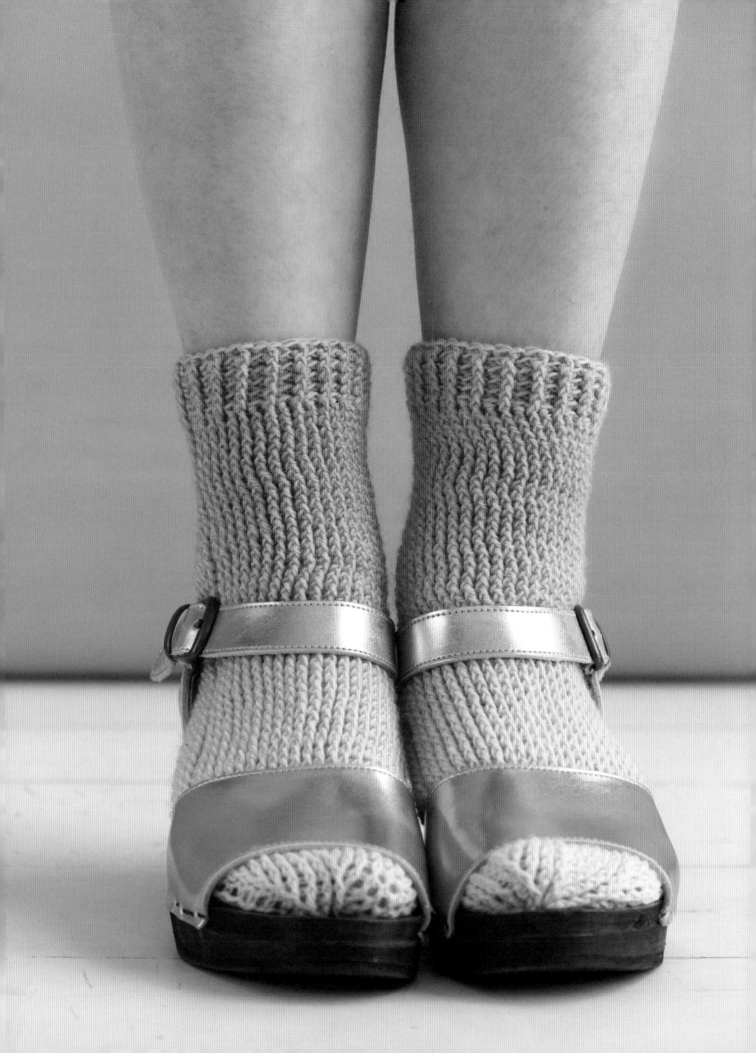

Rnds 47-53: Ch2, fpdc24, hdc1, fpdc23, sl st in first
fpdc. (48)

Rnds 54-59: Ch2, *fpdc1, bpdc1*, repeat * to *
around, sl st in first fpdc. (48)

Fasten off and weave in ends.


SIZE: MEDIUM

Rnd 1:    Start with a magic loop, ch2 (first ch2
doesn't count as first dc throughout), 6dc in
the loop, sl st in first dc. (6)

Rnd 2:    Ch2, 2fpdc in each stitch around, sl st in
first fpdc. (12)

Rnd 3:    Ch2, *fpdc1, 2fpdc in next stitch*, repeat
* to * 2 more times, hdc1, 2fpdc in next
stitch, repeat * to * 2 more times, sl st in
first fpdc. (18)

Rnd 4:    Ch2, *fpdc2, 2fpdc in next stitch*, repeat
* to * 2 more times, hdc1, fpdc1, 2fpdc in
next stitch, repeat * to * 2 more times, sl
st in first fpdc. (24)

Rnd 5:    Ch2, *fpdc3, 2fpdc in next stitch*, repeat
* to * 2 more times, hdc1, fpdc2, 2fpdc in
next stitch, repeat * to * 2 more times, sl
st in first fpdc. (30)

Rnd 6:    Ch2, *fpdc4, 2fpdc in next stitch*, repeat
* to * 2 more times, hdc1, fpdc3, 2fpdc in
next stitch, repeat * to * 2 more times, sl
st in first fpdc. (36)

Rnd 7:    Ch2, *fpdc5, 2fpdc in next stitch*, repeat
* to * 2 more times, hdc1, fpdc4, 2fpdc in
next stitch, repeat * to * 2 more times, sl
st in first fpdc. (42)

Rnd 8:    Ch2, *fpdc6, 2fpdc in next stitch*, repeat
* to * 2 more times, hdc1, fpdc5, 2fpdc in
next stitch, repeat * to * 2 more times, sl
st in first fpdc. (48)

Rnd 9:    Ch2, *fpdc7, 2fpdc in next stitch*, repeat
* to * 2 more times, hdc1, fpdc6, 2fpdc in
next stitch, repeat * to * 2 more times, sl
st in first fpdc. (54)

Rnds 10-37: Ch2, fpdc27, hdc1, fpdc26, sl st in first
fpdc. (54)

Rnd 38:   Ch2, 2fpdc in next stitch, fpdc25, 2fpdc
in next stitch, hdc1, fpdc26, sl st in first
fpdc. (56)

Rnd 39:   Ch2, fpdc1, 2fpdc in next stitch, fpdc25,
2fpdc in next stitch, fpdc1, hdc1, fpdc26,
sl st in first fpdc. (58)

Rnd 40:   Ch2, fpdc2, 2fpdc in next stitch, fpdc25,
2fpdc in next stitch, fpdc2, hdc1, fpdc26,
sl st in first fpdc. (60)

Rnd 41:   Ch2, fpdc3, 2fpdc in next stitch, fpdc25,
2fpdc in next stitch, fpdc3, hdc1, fpdc26,
sl st in first fpdc. (62)

Rnd 42:   Ch2, fpdc4, 2fpdc in next stitch, fpdc25,
2fpdc in next stitch, fpdc4, hdc1, fpdc26,
sl st in first fpdc. (64)

Rnd 43:   Ch2, fpdc5, 2fpdc in next stitch, fpdc25,
2fpdc in next stitch, fpdc5, hdc1, fpdc26,
sl st in first fpdc. (66)

Rnd 44:   Ch2, fpdc6, 2fpdc in next stitch, fpdc25,
2fpdc in next stitch, fpdc6, hdc1, fpdc26,
sl st in first fpdc. (68)

Rnd 45:   Ch2, fpdc7, 2fpdc in next stitch, fpdc25,
2fpdc in next stitch, fpdc7, hdc1, fpdc26,
sl st in first fpdc. (70)

Rnd 46:   Ch2, fpdc7, fpdc2tog, fpdc25, fpdc2tog,
fpdc7, hdc1, fpdc26, sl st in first fpdc.
(68)

Rnd 47:   Ch2, fpdc6, fpdc2tog, fpdc25, fpdc2tog,
fpdc6, hdc1, fpdc26, sl st in first fpdc.
(66)

Rnd 48:   Ch2, fpdc5, fpdc2tog, fpdc25, fpdc2tog,
fpdc5, hdc1, fpdc26, sl st in first fpdc.
(64)

Rnd 49:   Ch2, fpdc4, fpdc2tog, fpdc25, fpdc2tog,
fpdc4, hdc1, fpdc26, sl st in first fpdc.
(62)

Rnd 50:   Ch2, fpdc3, fpdc2tog, fpdc25, fpdc2tog,
fpdc3, hdc1, fpdc26, sl st in first fpdc.
(60)

Rnd 51:   Ch2, fpdc2, fpdc2tog, fpdc25, fpdc2tog,
fpdc2, hdc1, fpdc26, sl st in first fpdc.
(58)

Rnd 52:   Ch2, fpdc1, fpdc2tog, fpdc25, fpdc2tog,
fpdc1, hdc1, fpdc26, sl st in first fpdc.
(56)

Rnd 53:   Ch2, fpdc2tog, fpdc25, fpdc2tog, hdc1,
fpdc26, sl st in first fpdc. (54)

Rnds 54-61: Ch2, fpdc27, hdc1, fpdc26, sl st in first
fpdc. (54)

Rnds 62-69: Ch2, *fpdc1, bpdc1*, repeat * to *
around, sl st in first fpdc. (54)

Fasten off and weave in ends.

## SIZE: LARGE

Rnd 1: Start with a magic loop, ch2 (first ch2 doesn't count as first dc throughout), 6dc in the loop, sl st in first dc. (6)

Rnd 2: Ch2, 2fpdc in each stitch around, sl st in first fpdc. (12)

Rnd 3: Ch2, *fpdc1, 2fpdc in next stitch*, repeat * to * 2 more times, hdc1, 2fpdc in next stitch, repeat * to * 2 more times, sl st in first fpdc. (18)

Rnd 4: Ch2, *fpdc2, 2fpdc in next stitch*, repeat * to * 2 more times, hdc1, fpdc1, 2fpdc in next stitch, repeat * to * 2 more times, sl st in first fpdc. (24)

Rnd 5: Ch2, *fpdc3, 2fpdc in next stitch*, repeat * to * 2 more times, hdc1, fpdc2, 2fpdc in next stitch, repeat * to * 2 more times, sl st in first fpdc. (30)

Rnd 6: Ch2, *fpdc4, 2fpdc in next stitch*, repeat * to * 2 more times, hdc1, fpdc3, 2fpdc in next stitch, repeat * to * 2 more times, sl st in first fpdc. (36)

Rnd 7: Ch2, *fpdc5, 2fpdc in next stitch*, repeat * to * 2 more times, hdc1, fpdc4, 2fpdc in next stitch, repeat * to * 2 more times, sl st in first fpdc. (42)

Rnd 8: Ch2, *fpdc6, 2fpdc in next stitch*, repeat * to * 2 more times, hdc1, fpdc5, 2fpdc in next stitch, repeat * to * 2 more times, sl st in first fpdc. (48)

Rnd 9: Ch2, *fpdc7, 2fpdc in next stitch*, repeat * to * 2 more times, hdc1, fpdc6, 2fpdc in next stitch, repeat * to * 2 more times, sl st in first fpdc. (54)

Rnd 10: Ch2, *fpdc8, 2fpdc in next stitch*, repeat * to * 2 more times, hdc1, fpdc7, 2fpdc in next stitch, repeat * to * 2 more times, sl st in first fpdc. (60)

Rnds 11–42: Ch2, fpdc30, hdc1, fpdc29, sl st in first fpdc. (60)

Rnd 43: Ch2, 2fpdc in next stitch, fpdc28, 2fpdc in next stitch, hdc1, fpdc29, sl st in first fpdc. (62)

Rnd 44: Ch2, fpdc1, 2fpdc in next stitch, fpdc28, 2fpdc in next stitch, fpdc1, hdc1, fpdc29, sl st in first fpdc. (64)

Rnd 45: Ch2, fpdc2, 2fpdc in next stitch, fpdc28, 2fpdc in next stitch, fpdc2, hdc1, fpdc29, sl st in first fpdc. (66)

Rnd 46: Ch2, fpdc3, 2fpdc in next stitch, fpdc28, 2fpdc in next stitch, fpdc3, hdc1, fpdc29, sl st in first fpdc. (68)

Rnd 47: Ch2, fpdc4, 2fpdc in next stitch, fpdc28, 2fpdc in next stitch, fpdc4, hdc1, fpdc29, sl st in first fpdc. (70)

Rnd 48: Ch2, fpdc5, 2fpdc in next stitch, fpdc28, 2fpdc in next stitch, fpdc5, hdc1, fpdc20, sl st in first fpdc. (72)

Rnd 49: Ch2, fpdc6, 2fpdc in next stitch, fpdc28, 2fpdc in next stitch, fpdc6, hdc1, fpdc29, sl st in first fpdc. (74)

Rnd 50: Ch2, fpdc7, 2fpdc in next stitch, fpdc28, 2fpdc in next stitch, fpdc7, hdc1, fpdc29, sl st in first fpdc. (76)

Rnd 51: Ch2, fpdc8, 2fpdc in next stitch, fpdc28, 2fpdc in next stitch, fpdc8, hdc1, fpdc29, sl st in first fpdc. (78)

Rnd 52: Ch2, fpdc8, fpdc2tog, fpdc28, fpdc2tog, fpdc8, hdc1, fpdc29, sl st in first fpdc. (76)

Rnd 53: Ch2, fpdc7, fpdc2tog, fpdc28, fpdc2tog, fpdc7, hdc1, fpdc29, sl st in first fpdc. (74)

Rnd 54: Ch2, fpdc6, fpdc2tog, fpdc28, fpdc2tog, fpdc6, hdc1, fpdc29, sl st in first fpdc. (72)

Rnd 55: Ch2, fpdc5, fpdc2tog, fpdc28, fpdc2tog, fpdc5, hdc1, fpdc29, sl st in first fpdc. (70)

Rnd 56: Ch2, fpdc4, fpdc2tog, fpdc28, fpdc2tog, fpdc4, hdc1, fpdc29, sl st in first fpdc. (68)

Rnd 57: Ch2, fpdc3, fpdc2tog, fpdc28, fpdc2tog, fpdc3, hdc1, fpdc29, sl st in first fpdc. (66)

Rnd 58: Ch2, fpdc2, fpdc2tog, fpdc28, fpdc2tog, fpdc2, hdc1, fpdc29, sl st in first fpdc. (64)

Rnd 59: Ch2, fpdc1, fpdc2tog, fpdc28, fpdc2tog, fpdc1, hdc1, fpdc29, sl st in first fpdc. (62)

Rnd 60: Ch2, fpdc2tog, fpdc28, fpdc2tog, hdc1, fpdc29, sl st in first fpdc. (60)

Rnds 61–70: Ch2, fpdc30, hdc1, fpdc29, sl st in first fpdc. (60)

Rnds 71–79: Ch2, *fpdc1, bpdc1*, repeat * to * around, sl st in first fpdc. (60)

Fasten off and weave in ends.

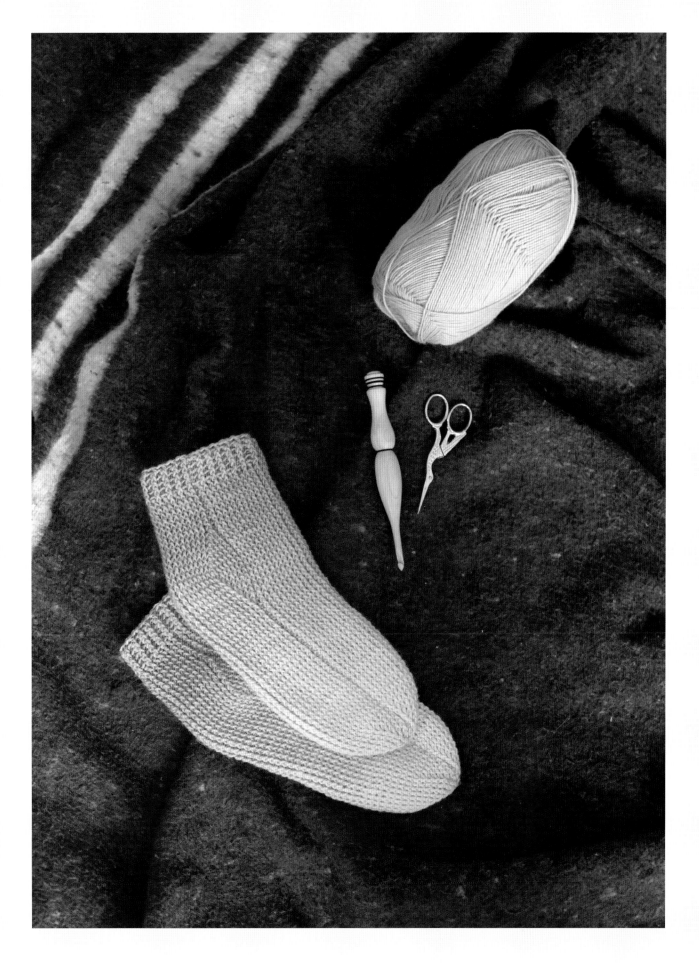

# armadillo

IT IS NOT DIFFICULT TO SEE WHERE THE NAME OF THESE SOCKS
COMES FROM. THE VARIATION IN THE DIRECTION OF THE STITCH
GIVES THIS PATTERN A VERY NICE AND PLAYFUL APPEARANCE.

For help in choosing the right size, see page 15.
For help in choosing the right hook size and checking gauge, see page 16.

## MATERIALS

**Yarn**

**Blue socks:**  Lang Yarn Jawoll Fingering, #1 super fine
weight (75% wool, 18% nylon/polyamide, 7%
acrylic; 230 yd./210 m per 1.76 oz./50 g); color
#0020

**Gray socks:**  Lang Yarns Super Soxx Cashmere Color, #1
super fine weight (75% superwash wool, 25%
nylon; 462 yd./422 m per 3.5 oz./100 g); color
#0020

**Hook**
US size G-6 (4 mm)

**Gauge**
5 fpdc wide and 4 rnds high = 0.7 in./2 cm

**Estimated total yarn required**
0–6 months: 230 yd./210 m; 12–24 months: 230 yd./210 m; 3–5
years: 460 yd./420 m; 6–10 years: 460 yd./420 m; Small: 689
yd./630 m; Medium: 689 yd./630 m

## ABBREVIATIONS

| | | |
|---|---|---|
| ∽ | **ch** | chain |
| Ŧ | **dc** | double crochet |
| Ŧ | **fpdc** | front post double crochet |
| Ŧ | **bpdc** | back post double crochet |
| ● | **sl st** | slip stitch |
| ⋏ | **fpdc2tog** | front post double crochet 2 together (1 stitch decreased) |
| ⋎ | **2 fpdc in the next stitch** | 2 fpdc in the same stitch (1 stitch increased) |
| ⋎ | **2bpdc in next stitch** | 2 bpdc in the same stitch (1 stitch increased) |

## SIZE: 0-6 MONTHS

**Rnd 1:** Start with a magic loop, ch2 (first ch2 doesn't count as first dc throughout), 6dc in the loop, sl st in first dc. (6)

**Rnd 2:** Ch2, 2fpdc in each stitch around, sl st in first fpdc. (12)

**Rnd 3:** Ch2, *fpdc1, 2fpdc in next stitch*, repeat * to * 2 more times, hdc1, 2bpdc in next st, ^bpdc1, 2bpdc in next st^, repeat ^ to ^ 1 more time, sl st in first fpdc. (18)

**Rnd 4:** Ch2, *fpdc2, 2fpdc in next stitch*, repeat * to * 2 more times, hdc1, bpdc1, 2bpdc in next st, ^bpdc2, 2bpdc in next st^, repeat ^ to ^ 1 more time, sl st in first fpdc. (24)

**Rnds 5-12:** Ch2, fpdc12, hdc1, bpdc11, sl st in first fpdc. (24)

**Rnd 13:** Ch2, 2fpdc in next stitch, fpdc10, 2fpdc in next stitch, hdc1, bpdc11, sl st in first fpdc. (26)

**Rnd 14:** Ch2, fpdc1, 2fpdc in next stitch, fpdc10, 2fpdc in next stitch, fpdc1, hdc1, bpdc11, sl st in first fpdc. (28)

**Rnd 15:** Ch2, fpdc2, 2fpdc in next stitch, fpdc10, 2fpdc in next stitch, fpdc2, hdc1, bpdc11, sl st in first fpdc. (30)

**Rnd 16:** Ch2, fpdc2, fpdc2tog, fpdc10, fpdc2tog, fpdc2, hdc1, bpdc11, sl st in first fpdc. (28)

**Rnd 17:** Ch2, fpdc1, fpdc2tog, fpdc10, fpdc2tog, fpdc1, hdc1, bpdc11, sl st in first fpdc. (26)

**Rnd 18:** Ch2, fpdc2tog, fpdc10, fpdc2tog, hdc1, bpdc11, sl st in first fpdc. (24)

**Rnds 19-21:** Ch2, fpdc12, hdc1, bpdc11, sl st in first fpdc. (24)

**Rnds 22-24:** Ch2, *fpdc1, bpdc1*, repeat * to * around, sl st in first fpdc. (24)

Fasten off and weave in ends.


## SIZE: 12-24 MONTHS

**Rnd 1:** Start with a magic loop, ch2 (first ch2 doesn't count as first dc throughout), 6dc in the loop, sl st in first dc. (6)

**Rnd 2:** Ch2, 2fpdc in each stitch around, sl st in first fpdc. (12)

**Rnd 3:** Ch2, *fpdc1, 2fpdc in next stitch*, repeat * to * 2 more times, hdc1, 2bpdc in next st, ^bpdc1, 2bpdc in next st^, repeat ^ to ^ 1 more time, sl st in first fpdc. (18)

**Rnd 4:** Ch2, *fpdc2, 2fpdc in next stitch*, repeat * to * 2 more times, hdc1, bpdc1, 2bpdc in next st, ^bpdc2, 2bpdc in next st^, repeat ^ to ^ 1 more time, sl st in first fpdc. (24)

**Rnd 5:** Ch2, *fpdc3, 2fpdc in next stitch*, repeat * to * 2 more times, hdc1, bpdc2, 2bpdc in next st, ^bpdc3, 2bpdc in next st^, repeat ^ to ^ 1 more time, sl st in first fpdc. (30)

**Rnds 6-17:** Ch2, fpdc15, hdc1, bpdc14, sl st in first fpdc. (30)

**Rnd 18:** Ch2, 2fpdc in next stitch, fpdc13, 2fpdc in next stitch, hdc1, bpdc14, sl st in first fpdc. (32)

**Rnd 19:** Ch2, fpdc1, 2fpdc in next stitch, fpdc13, 2fpdc in next stitch, fpdc1, hdc1, bpdc14, sl st in first fpdc. (34)

**Rnd 20:** Ch2, fpdc2, 2fpdc in next stitch, fpdc13, 2fpdc in next stitch, fpdc2, hdc1, bpdc14, sl st in first fpdc. (36)

**Rnd 21:** Ch2, fpdc3, 2fpdc in next stitch, fpdc13, 2fpdc in next stitch, fpdc3, hdc1, bpdc14, sl st in first fpdc. (38)

**Rnd 22:** Ch2, fpdc3, fpdc2tog, fpdc13, fpdc2tog, fpdc3, hdc1, bpdc14, sl st in first fpdc. (36)

**Rnd 23:** Ch2, fpdc2, fpdc2tog, fpdc13, fpdc2tog, fpdc2, hdc1, bpdc14, sl st in first fpdc. (34)

**Rnd 24:** Ch2, fpdc1, fpdc2tog, fpdc13, fpdc2tog, fpdc1, hdc1, bpdc14, sl st in first fpdc. (32)

**Rnd 25:** Ch2, fpdc2tog, fpdc13, fpdc2tog, hdc1, bpdc14, sl st in first fpdc. (30)

**Rnds 26-30:** Ch2, fpdc15, hdc1, bpdc14, sl st in first fpdc. (30)

**Rnds 31-34:** Ch2, *fpdc1, bpdc1*, repeat * to * around, sl st in first fpdc. (30)

Fasten off and weave in ends.


## SIZE: 3-5 YEARS

**Rnd 1:** Start with a magic loop, ch2 (first ch2 doesn't count as first dc throughout), 6dc in the loop, sl st in first dc. (6)

Rnd 2:  Ch2, 2fpdc in each stitch around, sl st in
first fpdc. (12)

Rnd 3:  Ch2, *fpdc1, 2fpdc in next stitch*, repeat
* to * 2 more times, hdc1, 2bpdc in next st,
^bpdc1, 2bpdc in next st^, repeat ^ to ^ 1
more time, sl st in first fpdc. (18)

Rnd 4:  Ch2, *fpdc2, 2fpdc in next stitch*, repeat
* to * 2 more times, hdc1, bpdc1, 2bpdc in
next st, ^bpdc2, 2bpdc in next st^, repeat ^
to ^ 1 more time, sl st in first fpdc. (24)

Rnd 5:  Ch2, *fpdc3, 2fpdc in next stitch*, repeat
* to * 2 more times, hdc1, bpdc2, 2bpdc in
next st, ^bpdc3, 2bpdc in next st^, repeat ^
to ^ 1 more time, sl st in first fpdc. (30)

Rnd 6:  Ch2, *fpdc4, 2fpdc in next stitch*, repeat
* to * 2 more times, hdc1, bpdc3, 2bpdc in
next st, ^bpdc4, 2bpdc in next st^, repeat ^
to ^ 1 more time, sl st in first fpdc. (36)

Rnds 7–22: Ch2, fpdc18, hdc1, bpdc17, sl st in first
fpdc. (36)

Rnd 23: Ch2, 2fpdc in next stitch, fpdc16, 2fpdc
in next stitch, hdc1, bpdc17, sl st in first
fpdc. (38)

Rnd 24: Ch2, fpdc1, 2fpdc in next stitch, fpdc16,
2fpdc in next stitch, fpdc1, hdc1, bpdc17,
sl st in first fpdc. (40)

Rnd 25: Ch2, fpdc2, 2fpdc in next stitch, fpdc16,
2fpdc in next stitch, fpdc2, hdc1, bpdc17,
sl st in first fpdc. (42)

Rnd 26: Ch2, fpdc3, 2fpdc in next stitch, fpdc16,
2fpdc in next stitch, fpdc3, hdc1, bpdc17,
sl st in first fpdc. (44)

Rnd 27: Ch2, fpdc4, 2fpdc in next stitch, fpdc16,
2fpdc in next stitch, fpdc4, hdc1, bpdc17,
sl st in first fpdc. (46)

Rnd 28: Ch2, fpdc4, fpdc2tog, fpdc16, fpdc2tog,
fpdc4, hdc1, bpdc17, sl st in first fpdc.
(44)

Rnd 29: Ch2, fpdc3, fpdc2tog, fpdc16, fpdc2tog,
fpdc3, hdc1, bpdc17, sl st in first fpdc.
(42)

Rnd 30: Ch2, fpdc2, fpdc2tog, fpdc16, fpdc2tog,
fpdc2, hdc1, bpdc17, sl st in first fpdc.
(40)

Rnd 31: Ch2, fpdc1, fpdc2tog, fpdc16, fpdc2tog,
fpdc1, hdc1, bpdc17, sl st in first fpdc.
(38)

Rnd 32: Ch2, fpdc2tog, fpdc16, fpdc2tog, hdc1,
bpdc17, sl st in first fpdc. (36)

Rnds 33–39: Ch2, fpdc18, hdc1, bpdc17, sl st in first
fpdc. (36)

Rnds 40–44: Ch2, *fpdc1, bpdc1*, repeat * to *
around, sl st in first fpdc. (36)

Fasten off and weave in ends.


SIZE: 6–10 YEARS

Rnd 1:  Start with a magic loop, ch2 (first ch2
doesn't count as first dc throughout), 6dc in
the loop, sl st in first dc. (6)

Rnd 2:  Ch2, 2fpdc in each stitch around, sl st in
first fpdc. (12)

Rnd 3:  Ch2, *fpdc1, 2fpdc in next stitch*, repeat
* to * 2 more times, hdc1, 2bpdc in next st,
^bpdc1, 2bpdc in next st^, repeat ^ to ^ 1
more time, sl st in first fpdc. (18)

Rnd 4:  Ch2, *fpdc2, 2fpdc in next stitch*, repeat
* to * 2 more times, hdc1, bpdc1, 2bpdc in
next st, ^bpdc2, 2bpdc in next st^, repeat ^
to ^ 1 more time, sl st in first fpdc. (24)

Rnd 5:  Ch2, *fpdc3, 2fpdc in next stitch*, repeat
* to * 2 more times, hdc1, bpdc2, 2bpdc in
next st, ^bpdc3, 2bpdc in next st^, repeat ^
to ^ 1 more time, sl st in first fpdc. (30)

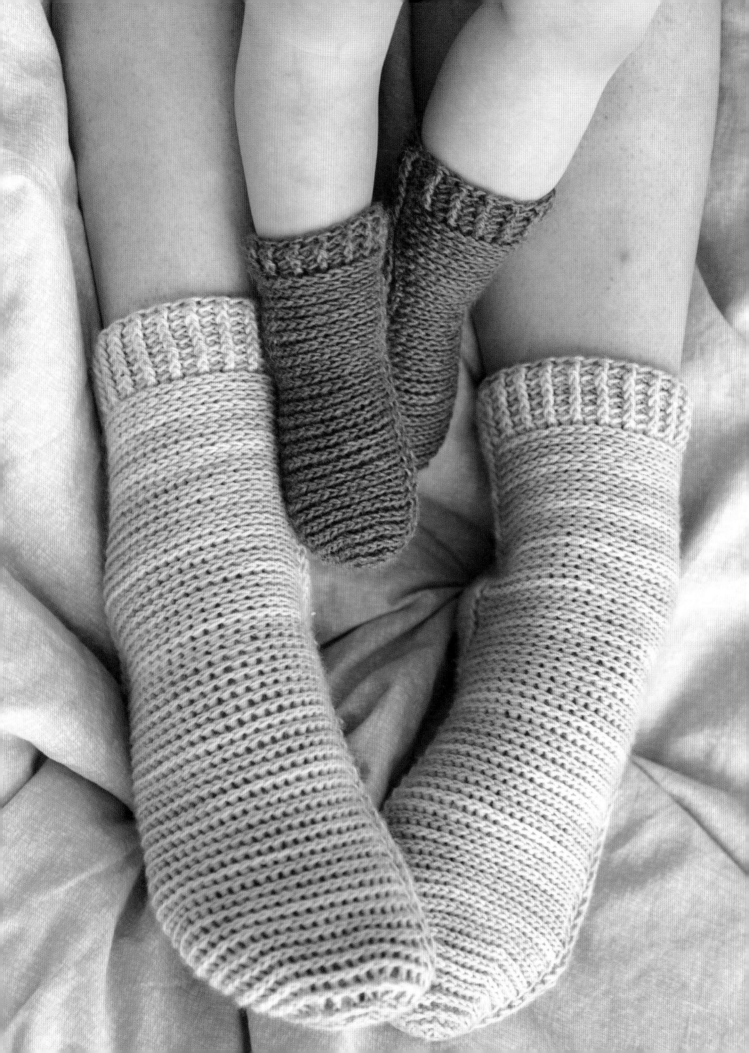

**Rnd 6:** Ch2, *fpdc4, 2fpdc in next stitch*, repeat
* to * 2 more times, hdc1, bpdc3, 2bpdc in
next st, ^bpdc4, 2bpdc in next st^, repeat ^
to ^ 1 more time, sl st in first fpdc. (36)

**Rnd 7:** Ch2, *fpdc5, 2fpdc in next stitch*, repeat
* to * 2 more times, hdc1, bpdc4, 2bpdc in
next st, ^bpdc5, 2bpdc in next st^, repeat ^
to ^ 1 more time, sl st in first fpdc. (42)

**Rnds 8–27:** Ch2, fpdc21, hdc1, bpdc20, sl st in first
fpdc. (42)

**Rnd 28:** Ch2, 2fpdc in next stitch, fpdc19, 2fpdc
in next stitch, hdc1, bpdc20, sl st in first
fpdc. (44)

**Rnd 29:** Ch2, fpdc1, 2fpdc in next stitch, fpdc19,
2fpdc in next stitch, fpdc1, hdc1, bpdc20,
sl st in first fpdc. (46)

**Rnd 30:** Ch2, fpdc2, 2fpdc in next stitch, fpdc19,
2fpdc in next stitch, fpdc2, hdc1, bpdc20,
sl st in first fpdc. (48)

**Rnd 31:** Ch2, fpdc3, 2fpdc in next stitch, fpdc19,
2fpdc in next stitch, fpdc3, hdc1, bpdc20,
sl st in first fpdc. (50)

**Rnd 32:** Ch2, fpdc4, 2fpdc in next stitch, fpdc19,
2fpdc in next stitch, fpdc4, hdc1, bpdc20,
sl st in first fpdc. (52)

**Rnd 33:** Ch2, fpdc5, 2fpdc in next stitch, fpdc19,
2fpdc in next stitch, fpdc5, hdc1, bpdc20,
sl st in first fpdc. (54)

**Rnd 34:** Ch2, fpdc5, fpdc2tog, fpdc19, fpdc2tog,
fpdc5, hdc1, bpdc20, sl st in first fpdc.
(52)

**Rnd 35:** Ch2, fpdc4, fpdc2tog, fpdc19, fpdc2tog,
fpdc4, hdc1, bpdc20, sl st in first fpdc.
(50)

**Rnd 36:** Ch2, fpdc3, fpdc2tog, fpdc19, fpdc2tog,
fpdc3, hdc1, bpdc20, sl st in first fpdc.
(48)

**Rnd 37:** Ch2, fpdc2, fpdc2tog, fpdc19, fpdc2tog,
fpdc2, hdc1, bpdc20, sl st in first fpdc.
(46)

**Rnd 38:** Ch2, fpdc1, fpdc2tog, fpdc19, fpdc2tog,
fpdc1, hdc1, bpdc20, sl st in first fpdc.
(44)

**Rnd 39:** Ch2, fpdc2tog, fpdc19, fpdc2tog, hdc1,
bpdc20, sl st in first fpdc. (42)

**Rnds 40–48:** Ch2, fpdc21, hdc1, bpdc20, sl st in first
fpdc. (42)

**Rnds 49–54:** Ch2, *fpdc1, bpdc1*, repeat * to *
around, sl st in first fpdc. (42)

Fasten off and weave in ends.

**SIZE: SMALL**

**Rnd 1:** Start with a magic loop, ch2 (first ch2
doesn't count as first dc throughout), 6dc in
the loop, sl st in first dc. (6)

**Rnd 2:** Ch2, 2fpdc in each stitch around, sl st in
first fpdc. (12)

**Rnd 3:** Ch2, *fpdc1, 2fpdc in next stitch*, repeat
* to * 2 more times, hdc1, 2bpdc in next st,
^bpdc1, 2bpdc in next st^, repeat ^ to ^ 1
more time, sl st in first fpdc. (18)

**Rnd 4:** Ch2, *fpdc2, 2fpdc in next stitch*, repeat
* to * 2 more times, hdc1, bpdc1, 2bpdc in
next st, ^bpdc2, 2bpdc in next st^, repeat ^
to ^ 1 more time, sl st in first fpdc. (24)

**Rnd 5:** Ch2, *fpdc3, 2fpdc in next stitch*, repeat
* to * 2 more times, hdc1, bpdc2, 2bpdc in
next st, ^bpdc3, 2bpdc in next st^, repeat ^
to ^ 1 more time, sl st in first fpdc. (30)

**Rnd 6:** Ch2, *fpdc4, 2fpdc in next stitch*, repeat
* to * 2 more times, hdc1, bpdc3, 2bpdc in
next st, ^bpdc4, 2bpdc in next st^, repeat ^
to ^ 1 more time, sl st in first fpdc. (36)

**Rnd 7:** Ch2, *fpdc5, 2fpdc in next stitch*, repeat
* to * 2 more times, hdc1, bpdc4, 2bpdc in
next st, ^bpdc5, 2bpdc in next st^, repeat ^
to ^ 1 more time, sl st in first fpdc. (42)

**Rnd 8:** Ch2, *fpdc6, 2fpdc in next stitch*, repeat
* to * 2 more times, hdc1, bpdc5, 2bpdc in
next st, ^bpdc6, 2bpdc in next st^, repeat ^
to ^ 1 more time, sl st in first fpdc. (48)

**Rnds 9–32:** Ch2, fpdc24, hdc1, bpdc23, sl st in first
fpdc. (48)

**Rnd 33:** Ch2, 2fpdc in next stitch, fpdc22, 2fpdc
in next stitch, hdc1, bpdc23, sl st in first
fpdc. (50)

**Rnd 34:** Ch2, fpdc1, 2fpdc in next stitch, fpdc22,
2fpdc in next stitch, fpdc1, hdc1, bpdc23,
sl st in first fpdc. (52)

**Rnd 35:** Ch2, fpdc2, 2fpdc in next stitch, fpdc22,
2fpdc in next stitch, fpdc2, hdc1, bpdc23,
sl st in first fpdc. (54)

**Rnd 36:** Ch2, fpdc3, 2fpdc in next stitch, fpdc22,
2fpdc in next stitch, fpdc3, hdc1, bpdc23,
sl st in first fpdc. (56)

**Rnd 37:** Ch2, fpdc4, 2fpdc in next stitch, fpdc22,
2fpdc in next stitch, fpdc4, hdc1, bpdc23,
sl st in first fpdc. (58)

Rnd 38: Ch2, fpdc5, 2fpdc in next stitch, fpdc22, 2fpdc in next stitch, fpdc5, hdc1, bpdc23, sl st in first fpdc. (60)

Rnd 39: Ch2, fpdc6, 2fpdc in next stitch, fpdc22, 2fpdc in next stitch, fpdc6, hdc1, bpdc23, sl st in first fpdc. (62)

Rnd 40: Ch2, fpdc6, fpdc2tog, fpdc22, fpdc2tog, fpdc1, hdc1, bpdc23, sl st in first fpdc. (60)

Rnd 41: Ch2, fpdc5, fpdc2tog, fpdc22, fpdc2tog, fpdc2, hdc1, bpdc23, sl st in first fpdc. (58)

Rnd 42: Ch2, fpdc4, fpdc2tog, fpdc22, fpdc2tog, fpdc3, hdc1, bpdc23, sl st in first fpdc. (56)

Rnd 43: Ch2, fpdc3, fpdc2tog, fpdc22, fpdc2tog, fpdc4, hdc1, bpdc23, sl st in first fpdc. (54)

Rnd 44: Ch2, fpdc2, fpdc2tog, fpdc22, fpdc2tog, fpdc5, hdc1, bpdc23, sl st in first fpdc. (52)

Rnd 45: Ch2, fpdc1, fpdc2tog, fpdc22, fpdc2tog, fpdc6, hdc1, bpdc23, sl st in first fpdc. (50)

Rnd 46: Ch2, fpdc2tog, fpdc22, fpdc2tog, hdc1, bpdc23, sl st in first fpdc. (48)

Rnds 47-57: Ch2, fpdc24, hdc1, bpdc23, sl st in first fpdc. (48)

Rnds 58-64: Ch2, *fpdc1, bpdc1*, repeat * to * around, sl st in first fpdc. (48)

Fasten off and weave in ends.


SIZE: MEDIUM

Rnd 1: Start with a magic loop, ch2 (first ch2 doesn't count as first dc throughout), 6dc in the loop, sl st in first dc. (6)

Rnd 2: Ch2, 2fpdc in each stitch around, sl st in first fpdc. (12)

Rnd 3: Ch2, *fpdc1, 2fpdc in next stitch*, repeat * to * 2 more times, hdc1, 2bpdc in next st, ^bpdc1, 2bpdc in next st^, repeat ^ to ^ 1 more time, sl st in first fpdc. (18)

Rnd 4: Ch2, *fpdc2, 2fpdc in next stitch*, repeat * to * 2 more times, hdc1, bpdc1, 2bpdc in next st, ^bpdc2, 2bpdc in next st^, repeat ^ to ^ 1 more time, sl st in first fpdc. (24)

Rnd 5: Ch2, *fpdc3, 2fpdc in next stitch*, repeat * to * 2 more times, hdc1, bpdc2, 2bpdc in next st, ^bpdc3, 2bpdc in next st^, repeat ^ to ^ 1 more time, sl st in first fpdc. (30)

Rnd 6: Ch2, *fpdc4, 2fpdc in next stitch*, repeat * to * 2 more times, hdc1, bpdc3, 2bpdc in next st, ^bpdc4, 2bpdc in next st^, repeat ^ to ^ 1 more time, sl st in first fpdc. (36)

Rnd 7: Ch2, *fpdc5, 2fpdc in next stitch*, repeat * to * 2 more times, hdc1, bpdc4, 2bpdc in next st, ^bpdc5, 2bpdc in next st^, repeat ^ to ^ 1 more time, sl st in first fpdc. (42)

Rnd 8: Ch2, *fpdc6, 2fpdc in next stitch*, repeat * to * 2 more times, hdc1, bpdc5, 2bpdc in next st, ^bpdc6, 2bpdc in next st^, repeat ^ to ^ 1 more time, sl st in first fpdc. (48)

Rnd 9: Ch2, *fpdc7, 2fpdc in next stitch*, repeat * to * 2 more times, hdc1, bpdc6, 2bpdc in next st, ^bpdc7, 2bpdc in next st^, repeat ^ to ^ 1 more time, sl st in first fpdc. (54)

Rnds 10-37: Ch2, fpdc27, hdc1, bpdc26, sl st in first fpdc. (54)

Rnd 38: Ch2, 2fpdc in next stitch, fpdc25, 2fpdc in next stitch, hdc1, bpdc26, sl st in first fpdc. (56)

Rnd 39: Ch2, fpdc1, 2fpdc in next stitch, fpdc25, 2fpdc in next stitch, fpdc1, hdc1, bpdc26, sl st in first fpdc. (58)

Rnd 40: Ch2, fpdc2, 2fpdc in next stitch, fpdc25, 2fpdc in next stitch, fpdc2, hdc1, bpdc26, sl st in first fpdc. (60)

Rnd 41: Ch2, fpdc3, 2fpdc in next stitch, fpdc25, 2fpdc in next stitch, fpdc3, hdc1, bpdc26, sl st in first fpdc. (62)

Rnd 42: Ch2, fpdc4, 2fpdc in next stitch, fpdc25, 2fpdc in next stitch, fpdc4, hdc1, bpdc26, sl st in first fpdc. (64)

Rnd 43: Ch2, fpdc5, 2fpdc in next stitch, fpdc25, 2fpdc in next stitch, fpdc5, hdc1, bpdc26, sl st in first fpdc. (66)

Rnd 44: Ch2, fpdc6, 2fpdc in next stitch, fpdc25, 2fpdc in next stitch, fpdc6, hdc1, bpdc26, sl st in first fpdc. (68)

Rnd 45: Ch2, fpdc7, 2fpdc in next stitch, fpdc25, 2fpdc in next stitch, fpdc7, hdc1, bpdc26, sl st in first fpdc. (70)

Rnd 46: Ch2, fpdc7, fpdc2tog, fpdc25, fpdc2tog, fpdc7, hdc1, bpdc26, sl st in first fpdc. (68)

Rnd 47: Ch2, fpdc6, fpdc2tog, fpdc25, fpdc2tog, fpdc6, hdc1, bpdc26, sl st in first fpdc. (66)

**Rnd 48:** Ch2, fpdc5, fpdc2tog, fpdc25, fpdc2tog, fpdc5, hdc1, bpdc26, sl st in first fpdc. (64)

**Rnd 49:** Ch2, fpdc4, fpdc2tog, fpdc25, fpdc2tog, fpdc4, hdc1, bpdc26, sl st in first fpdc. (62)

**Rnd 50:** Ch2, fpdc3, fpdc2tog, fpdc25, fpdc2tog, fpdc3, hdc1, bpdc26, sl st in first fpdc. (60)

**Rnd 51:** Ch2, fpdc2, fpdc2tog, fpdc25, fpdc2tog, fpdc2, hdc1, bpdc26, sl st in first fpdc. (58)

**Rnd 52:** Ch2, fpdc1, fpdc2tog, fpdc25, fpdc2tog, fpdc1, hdc1, bpdc26, sl st in first fpdc. (56)

**Rnd 53:** Ch2, fpdc2tog, fpdc25, fpdc2tog, hdc1, bpdc26, sl st in first fpdc. (54)

**Rnds 54-66:** Ch2, fpdc27, hdc1, bpdc26, sl st in first fpdc. (54)

**Rnds 67-74:** Ch2, *fpdc1, bpdc1*, repeat * to * around, sl st in first fpdc. (54)

Fasten off and weave in ends.

# butterfly

THIS ELEGANT SOCK HAS A BEAUTIFUL OPENWORK TOP AND CUFF.
IT IS SOMEWHAT THINNER AND LIGHTER THAN THE OTHER SOCKS,
AND IS FUN TO WEAR IN AN OPEN SHOE.

For help in choosing the right size, see page 15.
For help in choosing the right hook size and checking gauge, see page 16.

## MATERIALS

**Yarn**

**Blue socks:** Lana Grossa Meilenweit 100 Cotton Stretch, #1 super fine weight (41% cotton, 39% superwash wool, 13% nylon, 7% elastic; 503 yd./460 m per 3.5 oz./100 g); color #8060

**Pink socks:** Lang Yarns Super Soxx Cashmere Color, #1 super fine weight (75% superwash wool, 25% nylon; 462 yd./422 m per 3.5 oz./100 g); color #0021

**Hook**

US size G-6 (4 mm)

**Gauge**

5 fpdc wide and 4 rnds high = 0.7 in./2 cm

**Estimated total yarn required**

0–6 months: 230 yd./210 m; 12–24 months: 230 yd./210 m; 3–5 years: 460 yd./420 m; 6–10 years: 460 yd./420 m; Small: 460 yd./420 m; Medium: 460 yd./420 m

## ABBREVIATIONS

| | | |
|---|---|---|
| ⌒ | **ch** | chain |
| | **hdc** | half double crochet |
| | **dc** | double crochet |
| | **fpdc** | front post double crochet |
| ● | **sl st** | slip stitch |
| | **fpdc2tog** | front post double crochet 2 together (1 stitch decreased) |
| | **2 fpdc in the next stitch** | 2 fpdc in the same stitch (1 stitch increased) |
| | **2bpdc in next stitch** | 2 bpdc in the same stitch (1 stitch increased) |

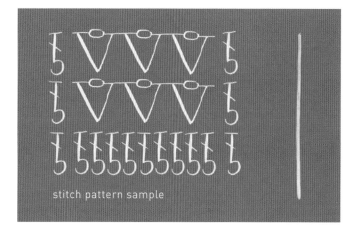

stitch pattern sample

**Rnd 1:** Start with a magic loop, ch2 (first ch2 doesn't count as first dc throughout), 6dc in the loop, sl st in first dc. (6)

**Rnd 2:** Ch2, 2fpdc in each stitch around, sl st in first fpdc. (12)

**Rnd 3:** Ch2, *fpdc1, 2fpdc in next stitch*, repeat * to * 2 more times, hdc1, 2fpdc in next stitch, ^fpdc1, 2fpdc in next stitch^, repeat ^ to ^ 1 more time, sl st in first fpdc. (18)

**Rnd 4:** Ch2, *fpdc2, 2fpdc in next stitch*, repeat * to * 2 more times, hdc1, fpdc1, 2fpdc in next stitch, ^fpdc2, 2fpdc in next stitch^, repeat ^ to ^ 1 more time, sl st in first fpdc. (24)

**Rnd 5:** Ch2, fpdc12, hdc1, fpdc11, sl st in first fpdc. (24)

**Rnd 6:** Ch2, fpdc12, hdc1, fpdc1, *skip 1 fpdc, 1hv-stitch in next fpdc, skip 1 fpdc*, repeat * to * to last fpdc (you should have 3 hv-stitches), fpdc1, sl st in first fpdc. (24)

**Rnds 7-12:** Ch2, fpdc12, hdc1, fpdc1, 1hv-stitch in each of the next hv-stitches (you'll always make these in the ch1-space) to last fpdc, fpdc1, sl st in first fpdc. (24)

**Rnd 13:** Ch2, 2fpdc in next stitch, fpdc10, 2fpdc in next stitch, hdc1, fpdc1, 1hv-stitch in each of the next hv-stitches to last fpdc, fpdc1, sl st in first fpdc. (26)

**Rnd 14:** Ch2, fpdc1, 2fpdc in next stitch, fpdc10, 2fpdc in next stitch, fpdc1, hdc1, fpdc1, 1hv-stitch in each of the next hv-stitches to last fpdc, fpdc1, sl st in first fpdc. (28)

**Rnd 15:** Ch2, fpdc2, 2fpdc in next stitch, fpdc10, 2fpdc in next stitch, fpdc2s, hdc1, fpdc1, 1hv-stitch in each of the next hv-stitches to last fpdc, fpdc1, sl st in first fpdc. (30)

**Rnd 16:** Ch2, fpdc2, fpdc2tog, fpdc10, fpdc2tog, fpdc2, hdc1, fpdc1, 1hv-stitch in each of the next hv-stitches to last fpdc, fpdc1, sl st in first fpdc. (28)

**Rnd 17:** Ch2, fpdc1, fpdc2tog, fpdc10, fpdc2tog, fpdc1, hdc1, fpdc1, 1hv-stitch in each of the next hv-stitches to last fpdc, fpdc1, sl st in first fpdc. (26)

**Rnd 18:** Ch2, fpdc2tog, fpdc10, fpdc2tog, hdc1, fpdc1, 1hv-stitch in each of the next hv-stitches to last fpdc, fpdc1, sl st in first fpdc. (24)

**Rnd 19:** Ch3, hdc1 in first fpdc (this counts as your first hv-stitch), *skip 2 fpdc, 1hv-stitch in next fpdc*, repeat to last 2 fpdc, skip 2 fpdc, 1hv-stitch in hdc, 1hv-stitch in each of the next hv-stitches to last fpdc, skip 1 fpdc, sl st around the first ch3. (8 hv-stitches)

**Rnd 20-23:** Ch3, hdc1 in first hv-stitch, 1hv-stitch in each of the next hv-stitches, sl st around the first ch3. (8 hv-stitches)

**Rnd 1:** Start with a magic loop, ch2 (first ch2 doesn't count as first dc throughout), 6dc in the loop, sl st in first dc. (6)

**Rnd 2:** Ch2, 2fpdc in each stitch around, sl st in first fpdc. (12)

**Rnd 3:** Ch2, *fpdc1, 2fpdc in next stitch*, repeat * to * 2 more times, hdc1, 2fpdc in next stitch, ^fpdc1, 2fpdc in next stitch^, repeat ^ to ^ 1 more time, sl st in first fpdc. (18)

**Rnd 4:** Ch2, *fpdc2, 2fpdc in next stitch*, repeat * to * 2 more times, hdc1, fpdc1, 2fpdc in next stitch, ^fpdc2, 2fpdc in next stitch^, repeat ^ to ^ 1 more time, sl st in first fpdc. (24)

**Rnd 5:** Ch2, *fpdc3, 2fpdc in next stitch*, repeat * to * 2 more times, hdc1, fpdc2, 2fpdc in next stitch, ^fpdc3, 2fpdc in next stitch^, repeat ^ to ^ 1 more time, sl st in first fpdc. (30)

**Rnds 6-7:** Ch2, fpdc15, hdc1, fpdc14, sl st in first fpdc. (30)

**Rnd 8:** Ch2, fpdc15, hdc1, fpdc1, *skip 1 fpdc, 1hv-stitch in next fpdc, skip 1 fpdc*, repeat * to * to last fpdc (you should have 4 hv-stitches), fpdc1, sl st in first fpdc. (30)

**Rnds 9-17:** Ch2, fpdc15, hdc1, fpdc1, *1hv-stitch in each of the next hv-stitches (you'll always make these in the ch1-space)*, repeat * to * to last fpdc, fpdc1, sl st in first fpdc. (30)

**Rnd 18:** Ch2, 2fpdc in next stitch, fpdc13, 2fpdc in next stitch, hdc1, fpdc1, 1hv-stitch in each of the next hv-stitches to last fpdc, fpdc1, sl st in first fpdc. (32)

**Rnd 19:** Ch2, fpdc1, 2fpdc in next stitch, fpdc13, 2fpdc in next stitch, fpdc1, hdc1, fpdc1,

1hv-stitch in each of the next hv-stitches to last fpdc, fpdc1, sl st in first fpdc. (34)

Rnd 20: Ch2, fpdc2, 2fpdc in next stitch, fpdc13, 2fpdc in next stitch, fpdc2, hdc1, fpdc1, 1hv-stitch in each of the next hv-stitches to last fpdc, fpdc1, sl st in first fpdc. (36)

Rnd 21: Ch2, fpdc3, 2fpdc in next stitch, fpdc13, 2fpdc in next stitch, fpdc3, hdc1, fpdc1, 1hv-stitch in each of the next hv-stitches to last fpdc, fpdc1, sl st in first fpdc. (38)

Rnd 22: Ch2, fpdc3, fpdc2tog, fpdc13, fpdc2tog, fpdc3, hdc1, fpdc1, 1hv-stitch in each of the next hv-stitches to last fpdc, fpdc1, sl st in first fpdc. (36)

Rnd 23: Ch2, fpdc2, fpdc2tog, fpdc13, fpdc2tog, fpdc2, hdc1, fpdc1, 1hv-stitch in each of the next hv-stitches to last fpdc, fpdc1, sl st in first fpdc. (34)

Rnd 24: Ch2, fpdc1, fpdc2tog, fpdc13, fpdc2tog, fpdc1, hdc1, fpdc1, 1hv-stitch in each of the next hv-stitches to last fpdc, fpdc1, sl st in first fpdc. (32)

Rnd 25: Ch2, fpdc2tog, fpdc13, fpdc2tog, hdc1, fpdc1, 1hv-stitch in each of the next hv-stitches to last fpdc, fpdc1, sl st in first fpdc. (30)

Rnd 26: Ch3, hdc1 in first fpdc (this counts as your first hv-stitch), *skip 2 fpdc, 1hv-stitch in next fpdc*, repeat to last 2 fpdc, skip 2 fpdc, 1hv-stitch in hdc, 1hv-stitch in each of the next hv-stitches to last fpdc, skip 1 fpdc, sl st around the first ch3. (10 hv-stitches)

Rnds 27-33: Ch3, hdc1 in first hv-stitch, 1hv-stitch in each of the next hv-stitches, sl st around the first ch3. (10 hv-stitches)

## SIZE: 3-5 YEARS

Rnd 1: Start with a magic loop, ch2 (first ch2 doesn't count as first dc throughout), 6dc in the loop, sl st in first dc. (6)

Rnd 2: Ch2, 2fpdc in each stitch around, sl st in first fpdc. (12)

Rnd 3: Ch2, *fpdc1, 2fpdc in next stitch*, repeat * to * 2 more times, hdc1, 2fpdc in next stitch, ^fpdc1, 2fpdc in next stitch^, repeat ^ to ^ 1 more time, sl st in first fpdc. (18)

Rnd 4: Ch2, *fpdc2, 2fpdc in next stitch*, repeat * to * 2 more times, hdc1, fpdc1, 2fpdc in next stitch, ^fpdc2, 2fpdc in next stitch^, repeat ^ to ^ 1 more time, sl st in first fpdc. (24)

Rnd 5: Ch2, *fpdc3, 2fpdc in next stitch*, repeat * to * 2 more times, hdc1, fpdc2, 2fpdc in next stitch, ^fpdc3, 2fpdc in next stitch^, repeat ^ to ^ 1 more time, sl st in first fpdc. (30)

Rnd 6: Ch2, *fpdc4, 2fpdc in next stitch*, repeat * to * 2 more times, hdc1, fpdc3, 2fpdc in next stitch, ^fpdc4, 2fpdc in next stitch^, repeat ^ to ^ 1 more time, sl st in first fpdc. (36)

Rnds 7-9: Ch2, fpdc18, hdc1, fpdc17, sl st in first fpdc. (36)

Rnd 10: Ch2, fpdc18, hdc1, fpdc1, *skip 1 fpdc, 1hv-stitch in next fpdc, skip 1 fpdc*, repeat * to * to last fpdc (you should have 5 hv-stitches), fpdc1, sl st in first fpdc. (36)

Rnds 11-22: Ch2, fpdc18, hdc1, fpdc1, *1hv-stitch in each of the next hv-stitches (you'll always make these in the ch1-space)*, repeat * to * to last fpdc, fpdc1, sl st in first fpdc. (36)

Rnd 23: Ch2, 2fpdc in next stitch, fpdc16, 2fpdc in next stitch, hdc1, fpdc1, 1hv-stitch in each of the next hv-stitches to last fpdc, fpdc1, sl st in first fpdc. (38)

Rnd 24: Ch2, fpdc1, 2fpdc in next stitch, fpdc16, 2fpdc in next stitch, fpdc1, hdc1, fpdc1, 1hv-stitch in each of the next hv-stitches to last fpdc, fpdc1, sl st in first fpdc. (40)

**Rnd 25:** Ch2, fpdc2, 2fpdc in next stitch, fpdc16, 2fpdc in next stitch, fpdc2, hdc1, fpdc1, 1hv-stitch in each of the next hv-stitches to last fpdc, fpdc1, sl st in first fpdc. (42)

**Rnd 26:** Ch2, fpdc3, 2fpdc in next stitch, fpdc16, 2fpdc in next stitch, fpdc3, hdc1, fpdc1, 1hv-stitch in each of the next hv-stitches to last fpdc, fpdc1, sl st in first fpdc. (44)

**Rnd 27:** Ch2, fpdc4, 2fpdc in next stitch, fpdc16, 2fpdc in next stitch, fpdc4, hdc1, fpdc1, 1hv-stitch in each of the next hv-stitches to last fpdc, fpdc1, sl st in first fpdc. (46)

**Rnd 28:** Ch2, fpdc4, fpdc2tog, fpdc16, fpdc2tog, fpdc4, hdc1, fpdc1, 1hv-stitch in each of the next hv-stitches to last fpdc, fpdc1, sl st in first fpdc. (44)

**Rnd 29:** Ch2, fpdc3, fpdc2tog, fpdc16, fpdc2tog, fpdc3, hdc1, fpdc1, 1hv-stitch in each of the next hv-stitches to last fpdc, fpdc1, sl st in first fpdc. (42)

**Rnd 30:** Ch2, fpdc2, fpdc2tog, fpdc16, fpdc2tog, fpdc2, hdc1, fpdc1, 1hv-stitch in each of the next hv-sittches to last fpdc, fpdc1, sl st in first fpdc. (40)

**Rnd 31:** Ch2, fpdc1, fpdc2tog, fpdc16, fpdc2tog, fpdc1, hdc1, fpdc1, 1hv-stitch in each of the next hv-stitches to last fpdc, fpdc1, sl st in first fpdc. (38)

**Rnd 32:** Ch2, fpdc2tog, fpdc16, fpdc2tog, hdc1, fpdc1, 1hv-stitch in each of the next hv-stitches to last fpdc, fpdc1, sl st in first fpdc. (36)

**Rnd 33:** Ch3, hdc1 in first fpdc (this counts as your first hv-stitch), *skip 2 fpdc, 1hv-stitch in next fpdc*, repeat to last 2 fpdc, skip 2 fpdc, 1hv-stitch in hdc, 1hv-stitch in each of the next hv-stitches to last fpdc, skip 1 fpdc, sl st around the first ch3. (12 hv-stitches)

**Rnds 34-43:** Ch3, hdc1 in first hv-stitch, 1hv-stitch in each of the next hv-stitches, sl st around the first ch3. (12 hv-stitches)

## SIZE: 6-10 YEARS

**Rnd 1:** Start with a magic loop, ch2 (first ch2 doesn't count as first dc throughout), 6dc in the loop, sl st in first dc. (6)

**Rnd 2:** Ch2, 2fpdc in each stitch around, sl st in first fpdc. (12)

**Rnd 3:** Ch2, *fpdc1, 2fpdc in next stitch*, repeat * to * 2 more times, hdc1, 2fpdc in next stitch, ^fpdc1, 2fpdc in next stitch^, repeat ^ to ^ 1 more time, sl st in first fpdc. (18)

**Rnd 4:** Ch2, *fpdc2, 2fpdc in next stitch*, repeat * to * 2 more times, hdc1, fpdc1, 2fpdc in next stitch, ^fpdc2, 2fpdc in next stitch^, repeat ^ to ^ 1 more time, sl st in first fpdc. (24)

**Rnd 5:** Ch2, *fpdc3, 2fpdc in next stitch*, repeat * to * 2 more times, hdc1, fpdc2, 2fpdc in next stitch, ^fpdc3, 2fpdc in next stitch^, repeat ^ to ^ 1 more time, sl st in first fpdc. (30)

**Rnd 6:** Ch2, *fpdc4, 2fpdc in next stitch*, repeat * to * 2 more times, hdc1, fpdc3, 2fpdc in next stitch, ^fpdc4, 2fpdc in next stitch^, repeat ^ to ^ 1 more time, sl st in first fpdc. (36)

**Rnd 7:** Ch2, *fpdc5, 2fpdc in next stitch*, repeat * to * 2 more times, hdc1, fpdc4, 2fpdc in next stitch, repeat * to * 2 more times, sl st in first fpdc. (42)

**Rnds 8-11:** Ch2, fpdc21, hdc1, fpdc20, sl st in first fpdc. (42)

**Rnd 12:** Ch2, fpdc21, hdc1, fpdc1, *skip 1 fpdc, 1hv-stitch in next fpdc, skip 1 fpdc*, repeat * to * to last fpdc (you should have 6 hv-stitches), fpdc1, sl st in first fpdc. (42)

**Rnds 13-27:** Ch2, fpdc21, hdc1, fpdc1, *1hv-stitch in each of the next hv-stitches (you'll always make these in the ch1-space)*, repeat * to * to last fpdc, fpdc1, sl st in first fpdc. (42)

**Rnd 28:** Ch2, 2fpdc in next stitch, fpdc19, 2fpdc in next stitch, hdc1, fpdc1, 1hv-stitch in each of the next hv-stitches to last fpdc, fpdc1, sl st in first fpdc. (44)

**Rnd 29:** Ch2, fpdc1, 2fpdc in next stitch, fpdc19, 2fpdc in next stitch, fpdc1, hdc1, fpdc1, 1hv-stitch in each of the next hv-stitches to last fpdc, fpdc1, sl st in first fpdc. (46)

**Rnd 30:** Ch2, fpdc2, 2fpdc in next stitch, fpdc19, 2fpdc in next stitch, fpdc2, hdc1, fpdc1, 1hv-stitch in each of the next hv-stitches to last fpdc, fpdc1, sl st in first fpdc. (48)

**Rnd 31:** Ch2, fpdc3, 2fpdc in next stitch, fpdc19, 2fpdc in next stitch, fpdc3, hdc1, fpdc1,

1hv-stitch in each of the next hv-stitches to last fpdc, fpdc1, sl st in first fpdc. (50)

**Rnd 32:** Ch2, fpdc4, 2fpdc in next stitch, fpdc19, 2fpdc in next stitch, fpdc4, hdc1, fpdc1, 1hv-stitch in each of the next hv-stitches to last fpdc, fpdc1, sl st in first fpdc. (52)

**Rnd 33:** Ch2, fpdc5, 2fpdc in next stitch, fpdc19, 2fpdc in next stitch, fpdc5, hdc1, fpdc1, 1hv-stitch in each of the next hv-stitches to last fpdc, fpdc1, sl st in first fpdc. (54)

**Rnd 34:** Ch2, fpdc5, fpdc2tog, fpdc19, fpdc2tog, fpdc5, hdc1, fpdc1, 1hv-stitch in each of the next hv-stitches to last fpdc, fpdc1, sl st in first fpdc. (52)

**Rnd 35:** Ch2, fpdc4, fpdc2tog, fpdc19, fpdc2tog, fpdc4, hdc1, fpdc1, 1hv-stitch in each of the next hv-stitches to last fpdc, fpdc1, sl st in first fpdc. (50)

**Rnd 36:** Ch2, fpdc3, fpdc2tog, fpdc19, fpdc2tog, fpdc3, hdc1, fpdc1, 1hv-stitch in each of the next hv-stitches to last fpdc, fpdc1, sl st in first fpdc. (48)

**Rnd 37:** Ch2, fpdc2, fpdc2tog, fpdc19, fpdc2tog, fpdc2, hdc1, fpdc1, 1hv-stitch in each of the next hv-stitches to last fpdc, fpdc1, sl st in first fpdc. (46)

**Rnd 38:** Ch2, fpdc1, fpdc2tog, fpdc19, fpdc2tog, fpdc1, hdc1, fpdc1, 1hv-stitch in each of the next hv-stitches to last fpdc, fpdc1, sl st in first fpdc. (44)

**Rnd 39:** Ch2, fpdc2tog, fpdc19, fpdc2tog, hdc1, fpdc1, 1hv-stitch in each of the next hv-stitches to last fpdc, fpdc1, sl st in first fpdc. (42)

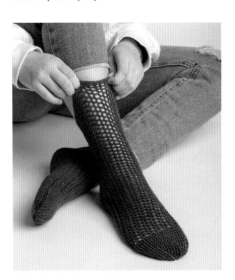

**Rnd 40:** Ch3, hdc1 in first fpdc (this counts as your first hv-stitch), *skip 2 fpdc, 1hv-stitch in next fpdc*, repeat to last 2 fpdc, skip 2 fpdc, 1hv-stitch in hdc, 1hv-stitch in each of the next hv-stitches to last fpdc, skip 1 fpdc, sl st around the first ch3. (14 hv-stitches)

**Rnds 41-53:** Ch3, hdc1 in first hv-stitch, 1hv-stitch in each of the next hv-stitches, sl st around the first ch3. (14 hv-stitches)

**SIZE: SMALL**

**Rnd 1:** Start with a magic loop, ch2 (first ch2 doesn't count as first dc throughout), 6dc in the loop, sl st in first dc. (6)

**Rnd 2:** Ch2, 2fpdc in each stitch around, sl st in first fpdc. (12)

**Rnd 3:** Ch2, *fpdc1, 2fpdc in next stitch*, repeat * to * 2 more times, hdc1, 2fpdc in next stitch, ^fpdc1, 2fpdc in next stitch^, repeat ^ to ^ 1 more time, sl st in first fpdc. (18)

**Rnd 4:** Ch2, *fpdc2, 2fpdc in next stitch*, repeat * to * 2 more times, hdc1, fpdc1, 2fpdc in next stitch, ^fpdc2, 2fpdc in next stitch^, repeat ^ to ^ 1 more time, sl st in first fpdc. (24)

**Rnd 5:** Ch2, *fpdc3, 2fpdc in next stitch*, repeat * to * 2 more times, hdc1, fpdc2, 2fpdc in next stitch, repeat * to * 2 more times, sl st in first fpdc. (30)

**Rnd 6:** Ch2, *fpdc4, 2fpdc in next stitch*, repeat * to * 2 more times, hdc1, fpdc3, 2fpdc in next stitch, ^fpdc4, 2fpdc in next stitch^, repeat ^ to ^ 1 more time, sl st in first fpdc. (36)

**Rnd 7:** Ch2, *fpdc5, 2fpdc in next stitch*, repeat * to * 2 more times, hdc1, fpdc4, 2fpdc in next stitch, ^fpdc5, 2fpdc in next stitch^, repeat ^ to ^ 1 more time, sl st in first fpdc. (42)

**Rnd 8:** Ch2, *fpdc6, 2fpdc in next stitch*, repeat * to * 2 more times, hdc1, fpdc5, 2fpdc in next stitch, ^fpdc6, 2fpdc in next stitch^, repeat ^ to ^ 1 more time, sl st in first fpdc. (48)

**Rnds 9-13:** Ch2, fpdc24, hdc1, fpdc23, sl st in first fpdc. (48)

**Rnd 14:** Ch2, fpdc24, hdc1, fpdc1, *skip 1 fpdc, 1hv-stitch in next fpdc, skip 1 fpdc*, repeat * to * to last fpdc (you should have 7 hv-stitches), fpdc1, sl st in first fpdc. (48)

**Rnds 15-32:** Ch2, fpdc24, hdc1, fpdc1, *1hv-stitch in each of the next hv-stitches (you'll always make these in the ch1-space)*, repeat * to * to last fpdc, fpdc1, sl st in first fpdc. (48)

**Rnd 33:** Ch2, 2fpdc in next stitch, fpdc22, 2fpdc in next stitch, hdc1, fpdc1, 1hv-stitch in each of the next hv-stitches to last fpdc, fpdc1, sl st in first fpdc. (50)

**Rnd 34:** Ch2, fpdc1, 2fpdc in next stitch, fpdc22, 2fpdc in next stitch, fpdc1, hdc1, fpdc1, 1hv-stitch in each of the next hv-stitches to last fpdc, fpdc1, sl st in first fpdc. (52)

**Rnd 35:** Ch2, fpdc2, 2fpdc in next stitch, fpdc22, 2fpdc in next stitch, fpdc2, hdc1, fpdc1, 1hv-stitch in each of the next hv-stitches to last fpdc, fpdc1, sl st in first fpdc. (54)

**Rnd 36:** Ch2, fpdc3, 2fpdc in next stitch, fpdc22, 2fpdc in next stitch, fpdc3, hdc1, fpdc1, 1hv-stitch in each of the next hv-stitches to last fpdc, fpdc1, sl st in first fpdc. (56)

**Rnd 37:** Ch2, fpdc4, 2fpdc in next stitch, fpdc22, 2fpdc in next stitch, fpdc4, hdc1, fpdc1, 1hv-stitch in each of the next hv-stitches to last fpdc, fpdc1, sl st in first fpdc. (58)

**Rnd 38:** Ch2, fpdc5, 2fpdc in next stitch, fpdc22, 2fpdc in next stitch, fpdc5, hdc1, fpdc1, 1hv-stitch in each of the next hv-stitches to last fpdc, fpdc1, sl st in first fpdc. (60)

**Rnd 39:** Ch2, fpdc6, 2fpdc in next stitch, fpdc22, 2fpdc in next stitch, fpdc6, hdc1, fpdc1, 1hv-stitch in each of the next hv-stitches to last fpdc, fpdc1, sl st in first fpdc. (62)

**Rnd 40:** Ch2, fpdc6, fpdc2tog, fpdc22, fpdc2tog, fpdc6, hdc1, fpdc1, 1hv-stitch in each of the next hv-stitches to last fpdc, fpdc1, sl st in first fpdc. (60)

**Rnd 41:** Ch2, fpdc5, fpdc2tog, fpdc22, fpdc2tog, fpdc5, hdc1, fpdc1, 1hv-stitch in each of the next hv-stitches to last fpdc, fpdc1, sl st in first fpdc. (58)

**Rnd 42:** Ch2, fpdc4, fpdc2tog, fpdc22, fpdc2tog, fpdc4, hdc1, fpdc1, 1hv-stitch in each of the next hv-stitches to last fpdc, fpdc1, sl st in first fpdc. (56)

**Rnd 43:** Ch2, fpdc3, fpdc2tog, fpdc22, fpdc2tog, fpdc3, hdc1, fpdc1, 1hv-stitch in each of the next hv-stitches to last fpdc, fpdc1, sl st in first fpdc. (54)

**Rnd 44:** Ch2, fpdc2, fpdc2tog, fpdc22, fpdc2tog, fpdc2, hdc1, fpdc1, 1hv-stitch in each of the next hv-stitches to last fpdc, fpdc1, sl st in first fpdc. (52)

**Rnd 45:** Ch2, fpdc1, fpdc2tog, fpdc22, fpdc2tog, fpdc1, hdc1, fpdc1, 1hv-stitch in each of the next hv-stitches to last fpdc, fpdc1, sl st in first fpdc. (50)

**Rnd 46:** Ch2, fpdc2tog, fpdc22, fpdc2tog, hdc1, fpdc1, 1hv-stitch in each of the next hv-stitches to last fpdc, fpdc1, sl st in first fpdc. (48)

**Rnd 47:** Ch3, hdc1 in first fpdc (this counts as your first hv-stitch), *skip 2 fpdc, 1hv-stitch in next fpdc*, repeat to last 2 fpdc, skip 2 fpdc, 1hv-stitch in hdc, 1hv-stitch in each of the next hv-stitches to last fpdc, skip 1 fpdc, sl st around the first ch3. (16 hv-stitches)

**Rnds 48-63:** Ch3, hdc1 in first hv-stitch, 1hv-stitch in each of the next hv-stitches, sl st around the first ch3. (16 hv-stitches)

## SIZE: MEDIUM

**Rnd 1:** Start with a magic loop, ch2 (first ch2 doesn't count as first dc throughout), 6dc in the loop, sl st in first dc. (6)

**Rnd 2:** Ch2, 2fpdc in each stitch around, sl st in first fpdc. (12)

**Rnd 3:** Ch2, *fpdc1, 2fpdc in next stitch*, repeat * to * 2 more times, hdc1, 2fpdc in next stitch, ^fpdc1, 2fpdc in next stitch^, repeat ^ to ^ 1 more time, sl st in first fpdc. (18)

**Rnd 4:** Ch2, *fpdc2, 2fpdc in next stitch*, repeat * to * 2 more times, hdc1, fpdc1, 2fpdc in next stitch, ^fpdc2, 2fpdc in next stitch^, repeat ^ to ^ 1 more time, sl st in first fpdc. (24)

**Rnd 5:** Ch2, *fpdc3, 2fpdc in next stitch*, repeat * to * 2 more times, hdc1, fpdc2, 2fpdc in next stitch, ^fpdc3, 2fpdc in next stitch^, repeat ^ to ^ 1 more time, sl st in first fpdc. (30)

**Rnd 6:** Ch2, *fpdc4, 2fpdc in next stitch*, repeat * to * 2 more times, hdc1, fpdc3, 2fpdc in next stitch, ^fpdc4, 2fpdc in next stitch^, repeat ^ to ^ 1 more time, sl st in first fpdc. (36)

**Rnd 7:** Ch2, *fpdc5, 2fpdc in next stitch*, repeat * to * 2 more times, hdc1, fpdc4, 2fpdc in next stitch, ^fpdc5, 2fpdc in next stitch^, repeat ^ to ^ 1 more time, sl st in first fpdc. (42)

**Rnd 8:** Ch2, *fpdc6, 2fpdc in next stitch*, repeat * to * 2 more times, hdc1, fpdc5, 2fpdc in next stitch, ^fpdc6, 2fpdc in next stitch^, repeat ^ to ^ 1 more time, sl st in first fpdc. (48)

**Rnd 9:** Ch2, *fpdc7, 2fpdc in next stitch*, repeat * to * 2 more times, hdc1, fpdc6, 2fpdc in next stitch, ^fpdc7, 2fpdc in next stitch^, repeat ^ to ^ 1 more time, sl st in first fpdc. (54)

**Rnds 10–15:** Ch2, fpdc27, hdc1, fpdc26, sl st in first fpdc. (54)

**Rnd 16:** Ch2, fpdc27, hdc1, fpdc1, *skip 1 fpdc, 1hv-stitch in next fpdc, skip 1 fpdc*, repeat * to * to last fpdc (you should have 8 hv-stitches), fpdc1, sl st in first fpdc. (54)

**Rnds 17–37:** Ch2, fpdc27, hdc1, fpdc1, *1hv-stitch in each of the next hv-stitches (you'll always make these in the ch1-space)*, repeat * to * to last fpdc, fpdc1, sl st in first fpdc. (54)

**Rnd 38:** Ch2, 2fpdc in next stitch, fpdc25, 2fpdc in next stitch, hdc1, fpdc1, 1hv-stitch in each of the next hv-stitches to last fpdc, fpdc1, sl st in first fpdc. (56)

**Rnd 39:** Ch2, fpdc1, 2fpdc in next stitch, fpdc25, 2fpdc in next stitch, fpdc1, hdc1, fpdc1, 1hv-stitch in each of the next hv-stitches to last fpdc, fpdc1, sl st in first fpdc. (58)

**Rnd 40:** Ch2, fpdc2, 2fpdc in next stitch, fpdc25, 2fpdc in next stitch, fpdc2, hdc1, fpdc1, 1hv-stitch in each of the next hv-stitches to last fpdc, fpdc1, sl st in first fpdc. (60)

**Rnd 41:** Ch2, fpdc3, 2fpdc in next stitch, fpdc25, 2fpdc in next stitch, fpdc3, hdc1, fpdc1, 1hv-stitch in each of the next hv-stitches to last fpdc, fpdc1, sl st in first fpdc. (62)

**Rnd 42:** Ch2, fpdc4, 2fpdc in next stitch, fpdc25, 2fpdc in next stitch, fpdc4, hdc1, fpdc1, 1hv-stitch in each of the next hv-stitches to last fpdc, fpdc1, sl st in first fpdc. (64)

**Rnd 43:** Ch2, fpdc5, 2fpdc in next stitch, fpdc25, 2fpdc in next stitch, fpdc5, hdc1, fpdc1, 1hv-stitch in each of the next hv-stitches to last fpdc, fpdc1, sl st in first fpdc. (66)

**Rnd 44:** Ch2, fpdc6, 2fpdc in next stitch, fpdc25, 2fpdc in next stitch, fpdc6, hdc1, fpdc1, 1hv-stitch in each of the next hv-stitches to last fpdc, fpdc1, sl st in first fpdc. (68)

**Rnd 45:** Ch2, fpdc7, 2fpdc in next stitch, fpdc25, 2fpdc in next stitch, fpdc7, hdc1, fpdc1, 1hv-stitch in each of the next hv-stitches to last fpdc, fpdc1, sl st in first fpdc. (70)

**Rnd 46:** Ch2, fpdc7, fpdc2tog, fpdc25, fpdc2tog, fpdc7, hdc1, fpdc1, 1hv-stitch in each of the next hv-stitches to last fpdc, fpdc1, sl st in first fpdc. (68)

**Rnd 47:** Ch2, fpdc6, fpdc2tog, fpdc25, fpdc2tog, fpdc6, hdc1, fpdc1, 1hv-stitch in each of the next hv-stitches to last fpdc, fpdc1, sl st in first fpdc. (66)

**Rnd 48:** Ch2, fpdc5, fpdc2tog, fpdc25, fpdc2tog, fpdc5, hdc1, fpdc1, 1hv-stitch in each of the next hv-stitches to last fpdc, fpdc1, sl st in first fpdc. (64)

**Rnd 49:** Ch2, fpdc4, fpdc2tog, fpdc25, fpdc2tog, fpdc4, hdc1, fpdc1, 1hv-stitch in each of the next hv-stitches to last fpdc, fpdc1, sl st in first fpdc. (62)

**Rnd 50:** Ch2, fpdc3, fpdc2tog, fpdc25, fpdc2tog, fpdc3, hdc1, fpdc1, 1hv-stitch in each of the next hv-stitches to last fpdc, fpdc1, sl st in first fpdc. (60)

**Rnd 51:** Ch2, fpdc2, fpdc2tog, fpdc25, fpdc2tog, fpdc2, hdc1, fpdc1, 1hv-stitch in each of the next hv-stitches to last fpdc, fpdc1, sl st in first fpdc. (58)

**Rnd 52:** Ch2, fpdc1, fpdc2tog, fpdc25, fpdc2tog, fpdc1, hdc1, fpdc1, 1hv-stitch in each of the next hv-stitches to last fpdc, fpdc1, sl st in first fpdc. (56)

**Rnd 53:** Ch2, fpdc2tog, fpdc25, fpdc2tog, hdc1, fpdc1, 1hv-stitch in each of the next hv-stitches to last fpdc, fpdc1, sl st in first fpdc. (54)

**Rnd 54:** Ch3, hdc1 in first fpdc (this counts as your first hv-stitch), *skip 2 fpdc, 1hv-stitch in next fpdc*, repeat to last 2 fpdc, skip 2 fpdc, 1hv-stitch in hdc, 1hv-stitch in each of the next hv-stitches to last fpdc, skip 1 fpdc, sl st around the first ch3. (18 hv-stitches)

**Rnds 55–66:** Ch3, hdc1 in first hv-stitch, 1hv-stitch in each of the next hv-stitches, sl st around the first ch3. (18 hv-stitches)

# locomotive

CHANGING COLORS AND ALTERNATING STITCHES GIVE
THIS SOCK A LIVELY LOOK. THE PATTERN IS EASY TO
LEARN AND FUN TO CROCHET!

For help in choosing the right size, see page 15.
For help in choosing the right hook size and checking gauge, see page 16.

## CHANGING COLOR

The best way to change colors is to complete the last step of the stitch before the color change with the new color. For these socks that means: When making the last fpdc before the color change, use the new color for the last yarn over and pull through (so the sl st doesn't count as the last stitch). In between the color changes, you don't have to cut the color you're not using. You can simply pick it up again when needed, but do not pull it tightly; leave the yarn loose enough to stretch a bit.

## MATERIALS

### Yarn
**Red/blue socks:**  Sheepjes Metropolis, #1 super fine weight (75% wool, 25% nylon; 218.7 yd./200 m per 1.75 oz./50 g); colors #045, #008, and #015

**Peach/green socks:**  Sheepjes Metropolis, #1 super fine weight (75% wool, 25% nylon; 218.7 yd./200 m per 1.75 oz./50 g) colors #047, #048, and #022

### Hook
US size G-6 (4 mm)

### Gauge
5 fpdc wide and 4 rnds high = 0.7 in./2 cm

### Estimated total yarn required
0–6 months: 230 yd./210 m; 12–24 months: 230 yd./210 m; 3–5 years: 460 yd./420 m; 6–10 years: 460 yd./420 m; Small: 689 yd./630 m; Medium: 689 yd./630 m

### ABBREVIATIONS

|  |  |  |
|---|---|---|
| ⬯ | **ch** | chain |
| ⊤ | **dc** | double crochet |
| ⌡ | **fpdc** | front post double crochet |
| ⌠ | **bpdc** | back post double crochet |
| ⬤ | **sl st** | slip stitch |
| Ⓐ | **fpdc2tog** | front post double crochet 2 together (1 stitch decreased) |
| Ⓥ | **2 fpdc in the next stitch** | 2 fpdc in the same stitch (1 stitch increased) |

**Rnd 1:** With color for toe, start with a magic loop, ch2 (first ch2 doesn't count as first dc throughout), 6dc in the loop, sl st in first dc. (6)

**Rnd 2:** Ch2, 2fpdc in each stitch around, sl st in first fpdc. (12)

**Rnd 3:** Ch2, *fpdc1, 2fpdc in next stitch*, repeat * to * 2 more times, hdc1, 2fpdc in next stitch, repeat * to * 2 more times, sl st in first fpdc. (18)

**Rnd 4:** Ch2, *fpdc2, 2fpdc in next stitch*, repeat * to * 2 more times, hdc1, fpdc1, 2fpdc in next stitch, repeat * to * 2 more times, sl st in first fpdc. (24)

**Rnds 5-7:** Ch2, fpdc12, hdc1, fpdc11, sl st in first fpdc. (24)

*From now on you'll change colors every rnd; you can cut the color for toe.*

**Rnd 8:** Continue with color for foot, ch2, fpdc12, hdc1, fpdc11, sl st in first fpdc. (24)

**Rnds 9-12:** Ch2, fpdc12, hdc1, fpdc1, bpdc2, *fpdc2, bpdc2*, repeat * to * to end, sl st in first fpdc. (24)

**Rnd 13:** Ch2, 2fpdc in next stitch, fpdc10, 2fpdc in next stitch, hdc1, fpdc1, bpdc2, *fpdc2, bpdc2*, repeat * to * to end, sl st in first fpdc. (26)

**Rnd 14:** Ch2, fpdc1, 2fpdc in next stitch, fpdc10, 2fpdc in next stitch, fpdc1, hdc1, fpdc1, bpdc2, *fpdc2, bpdc2*, repeat * to * to end, sl st in first fpdc. (28)

**Rnd 15:** Ch2, fpdc2, 2fpdc in next stitch, fpdc10, 2fpdc in next stitch, fpdc2, hdc1, fpdc1, bpdc2, *fpdc2, bpdc2*, repeat * to * to end, sl st in first fpdc. (30)

**Rnd 16:** Ch2, fpdc2, fpdc2tog, fpdc10, fpdc2tog, fpdc2, hdc1, fpdc1, bpdc2, *fpdc2, bpdc2*, repeat * to * to end, sl st in first fpdc. (28)

**Rnd 17:** Ch2, fpdc1, fpdc2tog, fpdc10, fpdc2tog, fpdc1, hdc1, fpdc1, bpdc2, *fpdc2, bpdc2*, repeat * to * to end, sl st in first fpdc. (26)

**Rnd 18:** Ch2, fpdc2tog, fpdc10, fpdc2tog, hdc1, fpdc1, bpdc2, *fpdc2, bpdc2*, repeat * to * to end, sl st in first fpdc. (24)

**Rnds 19-21:** Ch2, *fpdc2, bpdc2*, repeat * to * to end, sl st in first fpdc. (24)

*Continue with color of cuff; you can cut the colors for the foot.*

**Rnds 22-24:** Ch2, *fpdc2, bpdc2*, repeat * to * to end, sl st in first fpdc. (24)

Fasten off and weave in ends.

**Rnd 1:** With color for toe, start with a magic loop, ch2 (first ch2 doesn't count as first dc throughout), 6dc in the loop, sl st in first dc. (6)

**Rnd 2:** Ch2, 2fpdc in each stitch around, sl st in first fpdc. (12)

**Rnd 3:** Ch2, *fpdc1, 2fpdc in next stitch*, repeat * to * 2 more times, hdc1, 2fpdc in next stitch, repeat * to * 2 more times, sl st in first fpdc. (18)

**Rnd 4:** Ch2, *fpdc2, 2fpdc in next stitch*, repeat * to * 2 more times, hdc1, fpdc1, 2fpdc in next stitch, repeat * to * 2 more times, sl st in first fpdc. (24)

**Rnd 5:** Ch2, *fpdc3, 2fpdc in next stitch*, repeat * to * 2 more times, hdc1, fpdc2, 2fpdc in next stitch, repeat * to * 2 more times, sl st in first fpdc. (30)

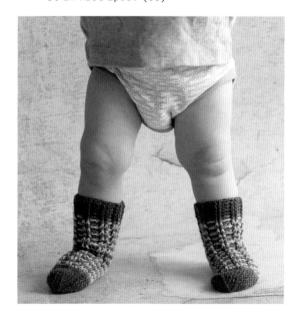

**Rnds 6-9:** Ch2, fpdc15, hdc1, fpdc14, sl st in first fpdc. (30)

*From now on you'll change colors every rnd; you can cut the color for toe.*

**Rnd 10:** Continue with color for foot, ch2, fpdc15, hdc1, fpdc14, sl st in first fpdc. (30)

**Rnds 11-17:** Ch2, fpdc15, hdc1, fpdc2, *bpdc2, fpdc2*, repeat * to * to end, sl st in first fpdc. (30)

**Rnd 18:** Ch2, 2fpdc in next stitch, fpdc13, 2fpdc in next stitch, hdc1, fpdc2, *bpdc2, fpdc2*, repeat * to * to end, sl st in first fpdc. (32)

**Rnd 19:** Ch2, fpdc1, 2fpdc in next stitch, fpdc13, 2fpdc in next stitch, fpdc1, hdc1, fpdc2, *bpdc2, fpdc2*, repeat * to * to end, sl st in first fpdc. (34)

**Rnd 20:** Ch2, fpdc2, 2fpdc in next stitch, fpdc13, 2fpdc in next stitch, fpdc2, hdc1, fpdc2, *bpdc2, fpdc2*, repeat * to * to end, sl st in first fpdc. (36)

**Rnd 21:** Ch2, fpdc3, 2fpdc in next stitch, fpdc13, 2fpdc in next stitch, fpdc3, hdc1, fpdc2, *bpdc2, fpdc2*, repeat * to * to end, sl st in first fpdc. (38)

**Rnd 22:** Ch2, fpdc3, fpdc2tog, fpdc13, fpdc2tog, fpdc3, hdc1, fpdc2, *bpdc2, fpdc2*, repeat * to * to end, sl st in first fpdc. (36)

**Rnd 23:** Ch2, fpdc2, fpdc2tog, fpdc13, fpdc2tog, fpdc2, hdc1, fpdc2, *bpdc2, fpdc2*, repeat * to * to end, sl st in first fpdc. (34)

**Rnd 24:** Ch2, fpdc1, fpdc2tog, fpdc13, fpdc2tog, fpdc1, hdc1, fpdc2, *bpdc2, fpdc2*, repeat * to * to end, sl st in first fpdc. (32)

**Rnd 25:** Ch2, fpdc2tog, fpdc13, fpdc2tog, hdc1 (place marker on this hdc), fpdc2, *bpdc2, fpdc2*, repeat * to * to end, sl st in first fpdc. (30)

**Rnds 26-30:** Ch2, bpdc1, fpdc2, *bpdc2, fpdc2*, repeat * to * to marker, bpdc1 in marked stitch and place marker in this bpdc, fpdc2, repeat * to * to end, sl st in first bpdc. (30)

*Continue with color of cuff; you can cut the colors for the foot.*

**Rnds 31-34:** Ch2, bpdc1, fpdc2, *bpdc2, fpdc2*, repeat * to * to marker, bpdc1 in marked stitch and place marker in this bpdc, fpdc2, repeat * to * to end, sl st in first bpdc. (30)
Fasten off and weave in ends.

**SIZE: 3-5 YEARS**

**Rnd 1:** With color for toe, start with a magic loop, ch2 (first ch2 doesn't count as first dc throughout), 6dc in the loop, sl st in first dc. (6)

**Rnd 2:** Ch2, 2fpdc in each stitch around, sl st in first fpdc. (12)

**Rnd 3:** Ch2, *fpdc1, 2fpdc in next stitch*, repeat * to * 2 more times, hdc1, 2fpdc in next stitch, repeat * to * 2 more times, sl st in first fpdc. (18)

**Rnd 4:** Ch2, *fpdc2, 2fpdc in next stitch*, repeat * to * 2 more times, hdc1, fpdc1, 2fpdc in next stitch, repeat * to * 2 more times, sl st in first fpdc. (24)

**Rnd 5:** Ch2, *fpdc3, 2fpdc in next stitch*, repeat * to * 2 more times, hdc1, fpdc2, 2fpdc in next stitch, repeat * to * 2 more times, sl st in first fpdc. (30)

**Rnd 6:** Ch2, *fpdc4, 2fpdc in next stitch*, repeat * to * 2 more times, hdc1, fpdc3, 2fpdc in next stitch, repeat * to * 2 more times, sl st in first fpdc. (36)

**Rnds 7-11:** Ch2, fpdc18, hdc1, fpdc17, sl st in first fpdc. (36)

*From now on you'll change colors every rnd; you can cut the color for toe.*

**Rnd 12:** Continue with color for foot, ch2, fpdc18, hdc1, fpdc17, sl st in first fpdc. (36)

**Rnds 13-22:** Ch2, fpdc18, hdc1, bpdc1, *fpdc2, bpdc2*, repeat * to * to end, sl st in first fpdc. (36)

**Rnd 23:** Ch2, 2fpdc in next stitch, fpdc16, 2fpdc in next stitch, hdc1, bpdc1, *fpdc2, bpdc2*, repeat * to * to end, sl st in first fpdc. (38)

**Rnd 24:** Ch2, fpdc1, 2fpdc in next stitch, fpdc16, 2fpdc in next stitch, fpdc1, hdc1, bpdc1, *fpdc2, bpdc2*, repeat * to * to end sl st in first fpdc. (40)

**Rnd 25:** Ch2, fpdc2, 2fpdc in next stitch, fpdc16, 2fpdc in next stitch, fpdc2, hdc1, bpdc1, *fpdc2, bpdc2*, repeat * to * to end, sl st in first fpdc. (42)

**Rnd 26:** Ch2, fpdc3, 2fpdc in next stitch, fpdc16, 2fpdc in next stitch, fpdc3, hdc1, bpdc1, *fpdc2, bpdc2*, repeat * to * to end, sl st in first fpdc. (44)

**Rnd 27:** Ch2, fpdc4, 2fpdc in next stitch, fpdc16, 2fpdc in next stitch, fpdc4, hdc1, bpdc1, *fpdc2, bpdc2*, repeat * to * to end, sl st in first fpdc. (46)

**Rnd 28:** Ch2, fpdc4, fpdc2tog, fpdc16, fpdc2tog, fpdc4, hdc1, bpdc1, *fpdc2, bpdc2*, repeat * to * to end, sl st in first fpdc. (44)

**Rnd 29:** Ch2, fpdc3, fpdc2tog, fpdc16, fpdc2tog, fpdc3, hdc1, bpdc1, *fpdc2, bpdc2*, repeat * to * to end, sl st in first fpdc. (42)

**Rnd 30:** Ch2, fpdc2, fpdc2tog, fpdc16, fpdc2tog, fpdc2, hdc1, bpdc1, *fpdc2, bpdc2*, repeat * to * to end, sl st in first fpdc. (40)

**Rnd 31:** Ch2, fpdc1, fpdc2tog, fpdc16, fpdc2tog, fpdc1, hdc1, bpdc1, *fpdc2, bpdc2*, repeat * to * to end, sl st in first fpdc. (38)

**Rnd 32:** Ch2, fpdc2tog, fpdc16, fpdc2tog, hdc1, bpdc1, *fpdc2, bpdc2*, repeat * to * to end, sl st in first fpdc. (36)

**Rnds 33–39:** Ch2, *fpdc2, bpdc2*, repeat * to * to end, sl st in first fpdc. (36)

Continue with color of cuff; you can cut the colors for the foot.

**Rnds 40–44:** Ch2, *fpdc2, bpdc2*, repeat * to * to end, sl st in first fpdc. (36)
Fasten off and weave in ends.


**SIZE: 6–10 YEARS**

**Rnd 1:** With color for toe, start with a magic loop, ch2 (first ch2 doesn't count as first dc throughout), 6dc in the loop, sl st in first dc. (6)

**Rnd 2:** Ch2, 2fpdc in each stitch around, sl st in first fpdc. (12)

**Rnd 3:** Ch2, *fpdc1, 2fpdc in next stitch*, repeat * to * 2 more times, hdc1, 2fpdc in next stitch, repeat * to * 2 more times, sl st in first fpdc. (18)

**Rnd 4:** Ch2, *fpdc2, 2fpdc in next stitch*, repeat * to * 2 more times, hdc1, fpdc1, 2fpdc in next stitch, repeat * to * 2 more times, sl st in first fpdc. (24)

**Rnd 5:** Ch2, *fpdc3, 2fpdc in next stitch*, repeat * to * 2 more times, hdc1, fpdc2, 2fpdc in next stitch, repeat * to * 2 more times, sl st in first fpdc. (30)

**Rnd 6:** Ch2, *fpdc4, 2fpdc in next stitch*, repeat * to * 2 more times, hdc1, fpdc3, 2fpdc in next stitch, repeat * to * 2 more times, sl st in first fpdc. (36)

**Rnd 7:** Ch2, *fpdc5, 2fpdc in next stitch*, repeat * to * 2 more times, hdc1, fpdc4, 2fpdc in next stitch, repeat * to * 2 more times, sl st in first fpdc. (42)

**Rnds 8–13:** Ch2, fpdc21, hdc1, fpdc20, sl st in first fpdc. (42)

From now on you'll change colors every rnd; you can cut the color for toe.

**Rnd 14:** Continue with color for foot, ch2, fpdc21, hdc1, fpdc20, sl st in first fpdc. (42)

**Rnds 15–27:** Ch2, fpdc21, hdc1, *fpdc1, bpdc2, fpdc1*, repeat * to * to end, sl st in first fpdc. (42)

**Rnd 28:** Ch2, 2fpdc in next stitch, fpdc19, 2fpdc in next stitch, hdc1, *fpdc1, bpdc2, fpdc1*, repeat * to * to end, sl st in first fpdc. (44)

**Rnd 29:** Ch2, fpdc1, 2fpdc in next stitch, fpdc19, 2fpdc in next stitch, fpdc1, hdc1, *fpdc1, bpdc2, fpdc1*, repeat * to * to end, sl st in first fpdc. (46)

**Rnd 30:** Ch2, fpdc2, 2fpdc in next stitch, fpdc19, 2fpdc in next stitch, fpdc2, hdc1, *fpdc1, bpdc2, fpdc1*, repeat * to * to end, sl st in first fpdc. (48)

**Rnd 31:** Ch2, fpdc3, 2fpdc in next stitch, fpdc19, 2fpdc in next stitch, fpdc3, hdc1, *fpdc1, bpdc2, fpdc1*, repeat * to * to end, sl st in first fpdc. (50)

**Rnd 32:** Ch2, fpdc4, 2fpdc in next stitch, fpdc19, 2fpdc in next stitch, fpdc4, hdc1, *fpdc1, bpdc2, fpdc1*, repeat * to * to end, sl st in first fpdc. (52)

**Rnd 33:** Ch2, fpdc5, 2fpdc in next stitch, fpdc19, 2fpdc in next stitch, fpdc5, hdc1, *fpdc1, bpdc2, fpdc1*, repeat * to * to end, sl st in first fpdc. (54)

**Rnd 34:** Ch2, fpdc5, fpdc2tog, fpdc19, fpdc2tog, fpdc5, hdc1, *fpdc1, bpdc2, fpdc1*, repeat * to * to end, sl st in first fpdc. (52)

**Rnd 35:** Ch2, fpdc4, fpdc2tog, fpdc19, fpdc2tog, fpdc4, hdc1, *fpdc1, bpdc2, fpdc1*, repeat * to * to end, sl st in first fpdc. (50)

**Rnd 36:** Ch2, fpdc3, fpdc2tog, fpdc19, fpdc2tog, fpdc3, hdc1, *fpdc1, bpdc2, fpdc1*, repeat * to * to end, sl st in first fpdc. (48)

**Rnd 37:** Ch2, fpdc2, fpdc2tog, fpdc19, fpdc2tog, fpdc2, hdc1, *fpdc1, bpdc2, fpdc1*, repeat * to * to end, sl st in first fpdc. (46)

**Rnd 38:** Ch2, fpdc1, fpdc2tog, fpdc19, fpdc2tog, fpdc1, hdc1, *fpdc1, bpdc2, fpdc1*, repeat * to * to end, sl st in first fpdc. (44)

**Rnd 39:** Ch2, fpdc2tog, fpdc19, fpdc2tog, hdc1 (place marker on this hdc), *fpdc1, bpdc2, fpdc1*, repeat * to * to end, sl st in first fpdc. (42)

**Rnds 40-48:** Ch2, bpdc1, *fpdc1, bpdc2, fpdc1*, repeat * to * marked stitch, bpdc in marked stitch, place marker in the bpdc you just made, *fpdc1, bpdc2, fpdc1, repeat * to * to end, sl st in first bpdc. (42)

Continue with color of cuff; you can cut the colors for the foot.

**Rnds 49-54:** Ch2, bpdc1, *fpdc1, bpdc2, fpdc1*, repeat * to * marked stitch, bpdc in marked stitch, place marker in the bpdc you just made, *fpdc1, bpdc2, fpdc1, repeat * to * to end, sl st in first bpdc. (42)

Fasten off and weave in ends.

**SIZE: SMALL**

---

**Rnd 1:** With color for toe, start with a magic loop, ch2 (first ch2 doesn't count as first dc throughout), 6dc in the loop, sl st in first dc. (6)

**Rnd 2:** Ch2, 2fpdc in each stitch around, sl st in first fpdc. (12)

**Rnd 3:** Ch2, *fpdc1, 2fpdc in next stitch*, repeat * to * 2 more times, hdc1, 2fpdc in next stitch, repeat * to * 2 more times, sl st in first fpdc. (18)

**Rnd 4:** Ch2, *fpdc2, 2fpdc in next stitch*, repeat * to * 2 more times, hdc1, fpdc1, 2fpdc in next stitch, repeat * to * 2 more times, sl st in first fpdc. (24)

**Rnd 5:** Ch2, *fpdc3, 2fpdc in next stitch*, repeat * to * 2 more times, hdc1, fpdc2, 2fpdc in next stitch, repeat * to * 2 more times, sl st in first fpdc. (30)

**Rnd 6:** Ch2, *fpdc4, 2fpdc in next stitch*, repeat * to * 2 more times, hdc1, fpdc3, 2fpdc in

next stitch, repeat * to * 2 more times, sl st in first fpdc. (36)

Rnd 7: Ch2, *fpdc5, 2fpdc in next stitch*, repeat * to * 2 more times, hdc1, fpdc4, 2fpdc in next stitch, repeat * to * 2 more times, sl st in first fpdc. (42)

Rnd 8: Ch2, *fpdc6, 2fpdc in next stitch*, repeat * to * 2 more times, hdc1, fpdc5, 2fpdc in next stitch, repeat * to * 2 more times, sl st in first fpdc. (48)

Rnds 9-15: Ch2, fpdc24, hdc1, fpdc23, sl st in first fpdc. (48)

From now on you'll change colors every rnd: you can cut the color for toe.

Rnd 16: Continue with color for foot, ch2, fpdc24, hdc1, fpdc23, sl st in first fpdc. (48)

Rnds 17-32: Ch2, fpdc24, hdc1, fpdc1, bpdc2, *fpdc2, bpdc2*, repeat * to * to end, sl st in first fpdc. (48)

Rnd 33: Ch2, 2fpdc in next stitch, fpdc22, 2fpdc in next stitch, hdc1, fpdc1, bpdc2, *fpdc2, bpdc2*, repeat * to * to end, sl st in first fpdc. (50)

Rnd 34: Ch2, fpdc1, 2fpdc in next stitch, fpdc22, 2fpdc in next stitch, fpdc1, hdc1, fpdc1, bpdc2, *fpdc2, bpdc2*, repeat * to * to end, sl st in first fpdc. (52)

Rnd 35: Ch2, fpdc2, 2fpdc in next stitch, fpdc22, 2fpdc in next stitch, fpdc2, hdc1, fpdc1, bpdc2, *fpdc2, bpdc2*, repeat * to * to end, sl st in first fpdc. (54)

Rnd 36: Ch2, fpdc3, 2fpdc in next stitch, fpdc22, 2fpdc in next stitch, fpdc3, hdc1, fpdc1, bpdc2, *fpdc2, bpdc2*, repeat * to * to end, sl st in first fpdc. (56)

Rnd 37: Ch2, fpdc4, 2fpdc in next stitch, fpdc22, 2fpdc in next stitch, fpdc4, hdc1, fpdc1, bpdc2, *fpdc2, bpdc2*, repeat * to * to end, sl st in first fpdc. (58)

Rnd 38: Ch2, fpdc5, 2fpdc in next stitch, fpdc22, 2fpdc in next stitch, fpdc5, hdc1, fpdc1, bpdc2, *fpdc2, bpdc2*, repeat * to * to end, sl st in first fpdc. (60)

Rnd 39: Ch2, fpdc6, 2fpdc in next stitch, fpdc22, 2fpdc in next stitch, fpdc6, hdc1, fpdc1, bpdc2, *fpdc2, bpdc2*, repeat * to * to end, sl st in first fpdc. (62)

Rnd 40: Ch2, fpdc6, fpdc2tog, fpdc22, fpdc2tog, fpdc6, hdc1, fpdc1, bpdc2, *fpdc2, bpdc2*, repeat * to * to end, sl st in first fpdc. (60)

Rnd 41: Ch2, fpdc5, fpdc2tog, fpdc22, fpdc2tog, fpdc5, hdc1, fpdc1, bpdc2, *fpdc2, bpdc2*, repeat * to * to end, sl st in first fpdc. (58)

Rnd 42: Ch2, fpdc4, fpdc2tog, fpdc22, fpdc2tog, fpdc4, hdc1, fpdc1, bpdc2, *fpdc2, bpdc2*, repeat * to * to end, sl st in first fpdc. (56)

Rnd 43: Ch2, fpdc3, fpdc2tog, fpdc22, fpdc2tog, fpdc3, hdc1, fpdc1, bpdc2, *fpdc2, bpdc2*, repeat * to * to end, sl st in first fpdc. (54)

Rnd 44: Ch2, fpdc2, fpdc2tog, fpdc22, fpdc2tog, fpdc2, hdc1, fpdc1, bpdc2, *fpdc2, bpdc2*, repeat * to * to end, sl st in first fpdc. (52)

Rnd 45: Ch2, fpdc1, fpdc2tog, fpdc22, fpdc2tog, fpdc1, hdc1, fpdc1, bpdc2, *fpdc2, bpdc2*, repeat * to * to end, sl st in first fpdc. (50)

Rnd 46: Ch2, fpdc2tog, fpdc22, fpdc2tog, hdc1, fpdc1, bpdc2, *fpdc2, bpdc2*, repeat * to * to end, sl st in first fpdc. (48)

Rnds 47-57: Ch2, *fpdc2, bpdc2*, repeat * to * to end, sl st in first fpdc. (48)

Continue with color of cuff; you can cut the colors for the foot.

Rnds 58-64: Ch2, *fpdc2, bpdc2*, repeat * to * to end, sl st in first fpdc. (36)

Fasten off and weave in ends.

## SIZE: MEDIUM

Rnd 1: With color for toe, start with a magic loop, ch2 (first ch2 doesn't count as first dc throughout), 6dc in the loop, sl st in first dc. (6)

Rnd 2: Ch2, 2fpdc in each stitch around, sl st in first fpdc. (12)

Rnd 3: Ch2, *fpdc1, 2fpdc in next stitch*, repeat * to * 2 more times, hdc1, 2fpdc in next stitch, repeat * to * 2 more times, sl st in first fpdc. (18)

Rnd 4: Ch2, *fpdc2, 2fpdc in next stitch*, repeat * to * 2 more times, hdc1, fpdc1, 2fpdc in next stitch, repeat * to * 2 more times, sl st in first fpdc. (24)

**Rnd 5:** Ch2, *fpdc3, 2fpdc in next stitch*, repeat * to * 2 more times, hdc1, fpdc2, 2fpdc in next stitch, repeat * to * 2 more times, sl st in first fpdc. (30)

**Rnd 6:** Ch2, *fpdc4, 2fpdc in next stitch*, repeat * to * 2 more times, hdc1, fpdc3, 2fpdc in next stitch, repeat * to * 2 more times, sl st in first fpdc. (36)

**Rnd 7:** Ch2, *fpdc5, 2fpdc in next stitch*, repeat * to * 2 more times, hdc1, fpdc4, 2fpdc in next stitch, repeat * to * 2 more times, sl st in first fpdc. (42)

**Rnd 8:** Ch2, *fpdc6, 2fpdc in next stitch*, repeat * to * 2 more times, hdc1, fpdc5, 2fpdc in next stitch, repeat * to * 2 more times, sl st in first fpdc. (48)

**Rnd 9:** Ch2, *fpdc7, 2fpdc in next stitch*, repeat * to * 2 more times, hdc1, fpdc6, 2fpdc in next stitch, repeat * to * 2 more times, sl st in first fpdc. (54)

**Rnds 10-17:** Ch2, fpdc27, hdc1, fpdc26, sl st in first fpdc. (54)

*From now on you'll change colors every rnd; you can cut the color for toe.*

**Rnd 18:** Continue with color for foot, ch2, fpdc27, hdc1, fpdc26, sl st in first fpdc. (54)

**Rnds 19-37:** Ch2, fpdc27, hdc1, fpdc2, *bpdc2, fpdc2*, repeat * to * to end, sl st in first fpdc. (54)

**Rnd 38:** Ch2, 2fpdc in next stitch, fpdc25, 2fpdc in next stitch, hdc1, fpdc2, *bpdc2, fpdc2*, repeat * to * to end, sl st in first fpdc. (56)

**Rnd 39:** Ch2, fpdc1, 2fpdc in next stitch, fpdc25, 2fpdc in next stitch, fpdc1, hdc1, fpdc2, *bpdc2, fpdc2*, repeat * to * to end, sl st in first fpdc. (58)

**Rnd 40:** Ch2, fpdc2, 2fpdc in next stitch, fpdc25, 2fpdc in next stitch, fpdc2, hdc1, fpdc2, *bpdc2, fpdc2*, repeat * to * to end, sl st in first fpdc. (60)

**Rnd 41:** Ch2, fpdc3, 2fpdc in next stitch, fpdc25, 2fpdc in next stitch, fpdc3, hdc1, fpdc2, *bpdc2, fpdc2*, repeat * to * to end, sl st in first fpdc. (62)

**Rnd 42:** Ch2, fpdc4, 2fpdc in next stitch, fpdc25, 2fpdc in next stitch, fpdc4, hdc1, fpdc2, *bpdc2, fpdc2*, repeat * to * to end, sl st in first fpdc. (64)

**Rnd 43:** Ch2, fpdc5, 2fpdc in next stitch, fpdc25, 2fpdc in next stitch, fpdc5, hdc1, fpdc2, *bpdc2, fpdc2*, repeat * to * to end, sl st in first fpdc. (66)

**Rnd 44:** Ch2, fpdc6, 2fpdc in next stitch, fpdc25, 2fpdc in next stitch, fpdc6, hdc1, fpdc2, *bpdc2, fpdc2*, repeat * to * to end, sl st in first fpdc. (68)

**Rnd 45:** Ch2, fpdc7, 2fpdc in next stitch, fpdc25, 2fpdc in next stitch, fpdc7, hdc1, fpdc2, *bpdc2, fpdc2*, repeat * to * to end, sl st in first fpdc. (70)

**Rnd 46:** Ch2, fpdc7, fpdc2tog, fpdc25, fpdc2tog, fpdc7, hdc1, fpdc2, *bpdc2, fpdc2*, repeat * to * to end, sl st in first fpdc. (68)

**Rnd 47:** Ch2, fpdc6, fpdc2tog, fpdc25, fpdc2tog, fpdc6, hdc1, fpdc2, *bpdc2, fpdc2*, repeat * to * to end, sl st in first fpdc. (66)

**Rnd 48:** Ch2, fpdc5, fpdc2tog, fpdc25, fpdc2tog, fpdc5, hdc1, fpdc2, *bpdc2, fpdc2*, repeat * to * to end, sl st in first fpdc. (64)

**Rnd 49:** Ch2, fpdc4, fpdc2tog, fpdc25, fpdc2tog, fpdc4, hdc1, fpdc2, *bpdc2, fpdc2*, repeat * to * to end, sl st in first fpdc. (62)

**Rnd 50:** Ch2, fpdc3, fpdc2tog, fpdc25, fpdc2tog, fpdc3, hdc1, fpdc2, *bpdc2, fpdc2*, repeat * to * to end, sl st in first fpdc. (60)

**Rnd 51:** Ch2, fpdc2, fpdc2tog, fpdc25, fpdc2tog, fpdc2, hdc1, fpdc2, *bpdc2, fpdc2*, repeat * to * to end, sl st in first fpdc. (58)

**Rnd 52:** Ch2, fpdc1, fpdc2tog, fpdc25, fpdc2tog, fpdc1, hdc1, fpdc2, *bpdc2, fpdc2*, repeat * to * to end, sl st in first fpdc. (56)

**Rnd 53:** Ch2, fpdc2tog, fpdc25, fpdc2tog, hdc1 (place marker on this hdc), fpdc2, *bpdc2, fpdc2*, repeat * to * to end, sl st in first fpdc. (54)

**Rnds 54-66:** Ch2, bpdc1, fpdc2, *bpdc2, fpdc2*, repeat * to * to marker, bpdc1 in marked stitch and place marker in this bpdc, fpdc2, repeat * to * to end, sl st in first bpdc. (54)

*Continue with color of cuff; you can cut the colors for the foot.*

**Rnds 67-74:** Ch2, bpdc1, fpdc2, *bpdc2, fpdc2*, repeat * to * to marker, bpdc1 in marked stitch and place marker in this bpdc, fpdc2, repeat * to * to end, sl st in first bpdc. (54)

Fasten off and weave in ends.

# coffee bean

THE STITCH PATTERN OF THESE SOCKS IS BASED ON THE KNITTED "COFFEE BEAN" STITCH—A BEAUTIFUL, CHIC PATTERN THAT IS VERY NICE TO CROCHET!

For help in choosing the right size, see page 15.
For help in choosing the right hook size and checking gauge, see page 16.

## MATERIALS

**Yarn**
**Blue socks:**   Lang Yarn Jawoll Twin, #1 super fine weight (75% wool, 25% nylon/polyamide; 230 yd./210 m per 1.76 oz./50 g); color #0501

**White/multicolor socks:**
Regia 4-Ply, #1 super fine weight (75% virgin wool, 25% polyamide; 459 yd./420 m per 3.5 oz./100 g); colors #05062 and #05025

**Hook**
US size G-6 (4 mm)

**Gauge**
5 fpdc wide and 4 rnds high = 0.7 in./2 cm

**Estimated total yarn required**
0–6 months: 230 yd./210 m; 12–24 months: 230 yd./210 m; 3–5 years: 460 yd./420 m; 6–10 years: 460 yd./420 m; Small: 460 yd./420 m; Medium: 689 yd./630 m

## ABBREVIATIONS

| | | |
|---|---|---|
| ⌒ | **ch** | chain |
| ⊤ | **dc** | double crochet |
| ⊥ | **fpdc** | front post double crochet |
| ⊥ | **bpdc** | back post double crochet |
| ● | **sl st** | slip stitch |
| ⊤ | **hdc** | half double crochet |
| V | **2fpdc in next stitch** | 2 fpdc in the same stitch (1 stitch increased) |
| A | **fpdc2tog** | front post double crochet 2 together (1 stitch decreased) |
| V | **3fpdc in next stitch** | 3 fpdc in the same stitch (2 stitches increased) |
| A | **fpdc3tog** | front post double crochet 3 together (2 stitch decreased) |

## SIZE: 0-6 MONTHS

**MOTIF 1:** Fpdc1, fpdc2tog, 3fpdc in next st, fpdc3tog, 3fpdc in next st, fpdc2tog, fpdc1.
**MOTIF 2:** Fpdc1, 2fpdc in next st, fpdc3tog, 3fpdc in next st, fpdc3tog, 2fpdc in next st, fpdc1.

**Rnd 1:** Start with a magic loop, ch2 (first ch2 doesn't count as first dc throughout), 6dc in the loop, sl st in first dc. (6)

**Rnd 2:** Ch2, 2fpdc in each stitch around, sl st in first fpdc. (12)

**Rnd 3:** Ch2, *fpdc1, 2fpdc in next st*, repeat * to * 2 more times, hdc1, 2fpdc in next stitch, repeat * to * 2 more times, sl st in first fpdc. (18)

**Rnd 4:** Ch2, *fpdc2, 2fpdc in next stitch*, repeat * to * 2 more times, hdc1, fpdc1, 2fpdc in next stitch, repeat * to * 2 more times, sl st in first fpdc. (24)

**Rnd 5:** Ch2, *fpdc12, hdc1, fpdc11, sl st in first fpdc. (24)

**Rnd 6:** Ch2, fpdc12, hdc1, Motif 1, sl st in first fpdc. (24)

**Rnd 7:** Ch2, fpdc12, hdc1, Motif 2, sl st in first fpdc. (24)

**Rnds 8-12:** Repeat Rnds 6-7; you'll end with Rnd 6.

**Rnd 13:** Ch2, 2fpdc in next stitch, fpdc10, 2fpdc in next stitch, hdc1, Motif 2, sl st in first fpdc. (26)

**Rnd 14:** Ch2, fpdc1, 2fpdc in next stitch, fpdc10, 2fpdc in next stitch, fpdc1, hdc1, Motif 1, sl st in first fpdc. (28)

**Rnd 15:** Ch2, fpdc2, 2fpdc in next stitch, fpdc10, 2fpdc in next stitch, fpdc2, hdc1, Motif 2, sl st in first fpdc. (30)

**Rnd 16:** Ch2, fpdc2, fpdc2tog, fpdc10, fpdc2tog, fpdc2, hdc1, Motif 1, sl st in first fpdc. (28)

**Rnd 17:** Ch2, fpdc1, fpdc2tog, fpdc10, fpdc2tog, fpdc1, hdc1, Motif 2, sl st in first fpdc. (26)

**Rnd 18:** Ch2, fpdc2tog, fpdc10, fpdc2tog, hdc1, Motif 1, sl st in first fpdc. (24)

**Rnd 19:** Ch2, bpdc1, Motif 2, hdc1, Motif 2, sl st in first bpdc. (24)

**Rnd 20:** Ch2, bpdc1, Motif 1, hdc1, Motif 1, sl st in first bpdc. (24)

**Rnd 21:** Repeat Rnd 19.

**Rnd 22:** Ch2, bpdc1, fpdc1 in each stitch to the hdc, hdc1, fpdc1 in each stitch to end, sl st in first bpdc. (24)

**Rnds 23–24:** Ch2, *bpdc1, fpdc1*, repeat * to * around, sl st in first bpdc. (24)

Fasten off and weave in ends.

**SIZE: 12–24 MONTHS**

**MOTIF 1:** Fpdc2tog, 3fpdc in next st, fpdc3tog, 3fpdc in next st, fpdc3tog, 3fpdc in next st, fpdc2tog, fpdc1.

**MOTIF 2:** 2fpdc in next st, fpdc3tog, 3fpdc in next st, fpdc3tog, 3fpdc in next st, fpdc3tog, 2fpdc in next st, fpdc1.

**Rnd 1:** Start with a magic loop, ch2 (first ch2 doesn't count as first dc throughout), 6dc in the loop, sl st in first dc. (6)

**Rnd 2:** Ch2, 2fpdc in each stitch around, sl st in first fpdc. (12)

**Rnd 3:** Ch2, *fpdc1, 2fpdc in next stitch*, repeat * to * 2 more times, hdc1, 2fpdc in next stitch, repeat * to * 2 more times, sl st in first fpdc. (18)

**Rnd 4:** Ch2, *fpdc2, 2fpdc in next stitch*, repeat * to * 2 more times, hdc1, fpdc1, 2fpdc in next stitch, repeat * to * 2 more times, sl st in first fpdc. (24)

**Rnd 5:** Ch2, *fpdc3, 2fpdc in next stitch*, repeat * to * 2 more times, hdc1, fpdc2, 2fpdc in next stitch, repeat * to * 2 more times, sl st in first fpdc. (30)

**Rnds 6–7:** Ch2, fpdc15, hdc1, fpdc14, sl st in first fpdc. (30)

**Rnd 8:** Ch2, fpdc15, hdc1, Motif 1, sl st in first fpdc. (30)

**Rnd 9:** Ch2, fpdc15, hdc1, Motif 2, sl st in first fpdc. (30)

**Rnds 10–17:** Repeat Rnds 8–9.

**Rnd 18:** Ch2, 2fpdc in next stitch, fpdc13, 2fpdc in next stitch, hdc1, Motif 1, sl st in first fpdc. (32)

**Rnd 19:** Ch2, fpdc1, 2fpdc in next stitch, fpdc13, 2fpdc in next stitch, fpdc1, hdc1, Motif 2, sl st in first fpdc. (34)

**Rnd 20:** Ch2, fpdc2, 2fpdc in next stitch, fpdc13, 2fpdc in next stitch, fpdc2, hdc1, Motif 1, sl st in first fpdc (36)

**Rnd 21:** Ch2, fpdc3, 2fpdc in next stitch, fpdc13, 2fpdc in next stitch, fpdc3, hdc1, Motif 2, sl st in first fpdc. (38)

**Rnd 22:** Ch2, fpdc3, fpdc2tog, fpdc13, fpdc2tog, fpdc3, hdc1, Motif 1, sl st in first fpdc. (36)

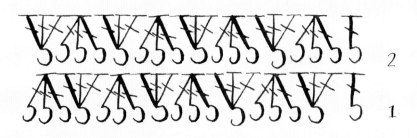

2

1

Rnd 23: Ch2, fpdc2, fpdc2tog, fpdc13, fpdc2tog,
fpdc2, hdc1, Motif 2, sl st in first fpdc.
(34)

Rnd 24: Ch2, fpdc1, fpdc2tog, fpdc13, fpdc2tog,
fpdc1, hdc1, Motif 1, sl st in first fpdc.
(32)

Rnd 25: Ch2, fpdc2tog, fpdc13, fpdc2tog, hdc1,
Motif 2, sl st in first fpdc. (30)

Rnd 26: Ch2, bpdc1, Motif 1, hdc1, Motif 1, sl st in
first bpdc. (30)

Rnd 27: Ch2, bpdc1, Motif 2, hdc1, Motif 2, sl st in
first bpdc. (30)

Rnds 28-29: Repeat Rnds 26-27.

Rnd 30: Ch2, bpdc1, fpdc1 in each stitch to the hdc,
hdc1, fpdc1 in each stitch to end, sl st in
first bpdc. (30)

Rnds 31-32: Ch2, *bpdc1, fpdc1*, repeat * to *
around, sl st in first bpdc. (30)

Fasten off and weave in ends.


SIZE: 3-5 YEARS


MOTIF 1: Fpdc1, *3fpdc in next st, fpdc3tog*,
repeat * to * to end.

MOTIF 2: Fpdc1, *fpdc3tog, 3fpdc in next st*,
repeat * to * to end.

Rnd 1: Start with a magic loop, ch2 (first ch2
doesn't count as first dc throughout), 6dc in
the loop, sl st in first dc. (6)

Rnd 2: Ch2, 2fpdc in each stitch around, sl st in
first fpdc. (12)

Rnd 3: Ch2, *fpdc1, 2fpdc in next stitch*, repeat
* to * 2 more times, hdc1, 2fpdc in next
stitch, repeat * to * 2 more times, sl st in
first fpdc. (18)

Rnd 4: Ch2, *fpdc2, 2fpdc in next stitch*, repeat
* to * 2 more times, hdc1, fpdc1, 2fpdc in
next stitch, repeat * to * 2 more times, sl
st in first fpdc. (24)

Rnd 5: Ch2, *fpdc3, 2fpdc in next stitch*, repeat
* to * 2 more times, hdc1, fpdc2, 2fpdc in
next stitch, repeat * to * 2 more times, sl
st in first fpdc. (30)

Rnd 6: Ch2, *fpdc4, 2fpdc in next stitch*, repeat
* to * 2 more times, hdc1, fpdc3, 2fpdc in
next stitch, repeat * to * 2 more times, sl
st in first fpdc. (36)

Rnds 7-9: Ch2, fpdc18, hdc1, fpdc17, sl st in first
fpdc. (36)

Rnd 10: Ch2, fpdc18, hdc1, Motif 1, sl st in first
fpdc. (36)

Rnd 11: Ch2, fpdc18, hdc1, Motif 2, sl st in first
fpdc. (36)

Rnds 12-21: Repeat Rnds 10-11.

Rnd 22: Ch2, 2fpdc in next stitch, fpdc16, 2fpdc in
next stitch, hdc1, Motif 1, sl st in first
fpdc. (38)

Rnd 23: Ch2, fpdc1, 2fpdc in next stitch, fpdc16,
2fpdc in next stitch, fpdc1, hdc1, Motif 2,
sl st in first fpdc. (40)

Rnd 24: Ch2, fpdc2, 2fpdc in next stitch, fpdc16,
2fpdc in next stitch, fpdc2, hdc1, Motif 1,
sl st in first fpdc. (42)

Rnd 25: Ch2, fpdc3, 2fpdc in next stitch, fpdc16,
2fpdc in next stitch, fpdc3, hdc1, Motif 2,
sl st in first fpdc. (44)

**Rnd 26:** Ch2, fpdc4, 2fpdc in next stitch, fpdc16, 2fpdc in next stitch, fpdc4, hdc1, Motif 1, sl st in first fpdc. (46)

**Rnd 27:** Ch2, fpdc4, fpdc2tog, fpdc16, fpdc2tog, fpdc4, hdc1, Motif 2, sl st in first fpdc. (44)

**Rnd 28:** Ch2, fpdc3, fpdc2tog, fpdc16, fpdc2tog, fpdc3, hdc1, Motif 1, sl st in first fpdc. (42)

**Rnd 29:** Ch2, fpdc2, fpdc2tog, fpdc16, fpdc2tog, fpdc2, hdc1, Motif 2, sl st in first fpdc. (40)

**Rnd 30:** Ch2, fpdc1, fpdc2tog, fpdc16, fpdc2tog, fpdc1, hdc1, Motif 1, sl st in first fpdc. (38)

**Rnd 31:** Ch2, fpdc2tog, fpdc16, fpdc2tog, hdc1, Motif 2, sl st in first fpdc. (36)

**Rnd 32:** Ch2, bpdc1, Motif 1, hdc1, Motif 1, sl st in first bpdc. (36)

**Rnd 33:** Ch2, bpdc1, Motif 2, hdc1, Motif 2, sl st in first bpdc. (36)

**Rnds 34-37:** Repeat Rnds 32-33.

**Rnd 38:** Ch2, bpdc1, fpdc1 in each stitch to the hdc, hdc1, fpdc1 in each stitch to end, sl st in first bpdc. (36)

**Rnds 39-40:** Ch2, *bpdc1, fpdc1*, repeat * to * around, sl st in first bpdc. (36)

Fasten off and weave in ends.

**SIZE: 6-10 YEARS**

**MOTIF 1:** *3fpdc in next st, fpdc3tog*, repeat * to * to end.

**MOTIF 2:** *Fpdc3tog, 3fpdc in next st*, repeat * to * to end.

**Rnd 1:** Start with a magic loop, ch2 (first ch2 doesn't count as first dc throughout), 6dc in the loop, sl st in first dc. (6)

**Rnd 2:** Ch2, 2fpdc in each stitch around, sl st in first fpdc. (12)

**Rnd 3:** Ch2, *fpdc1, 2fpdc in next stitch*, repeat * to * 2 more times, hdc1, 2fpdc in next stitch, repeat * to * 2 more times, sl st in first fpdc. (18)

**Rnd 4:** Ch2, *fpdc2, 2fpdc in next stitch*, repeat * to * 2 more times, hdc1, fpdc1, 2fpdc in next stitch, repeat * to * 2 more times, sl st in first fpdc. (24)

**Rnd 5:** Ch2, *fpdc3, 2fpdc in next stitch*, repeat * to * 2 more times, hdc1, fpdc2, 2fpdc in next stitch, repeat * to * 2 more times, sl st in first fpdc. (30)

**Rnd 6:** Ch2, *fpdc4, 2fpdc in next stitch*, repeat * to * 2 more times, hdc1, fpdc3, 2fpdc in next stitch, repeat * to * 2 more times, sl st in first fpdc. (36)

**Rnd 7:** Ch2, *fpdc5, 2fpdc in next stitch*, repeat * to * 2 more times, hdc1, fpdc4, 2fpdc in next stitch, repeat * to * 2 more times, sl st in first fpdc. (42)

**Rnds 8-11:** Ch2, fpdc21, hdc1, fpdc20, sl st in first fpdc. (42)

**Rnd 12:** Ch2, fpdc21, hdc1, Motif 1, sl st in first fpdc. (42)

**Rnd 13:** Ch2, fpdc21, hdc1, Motif 2, sl st in first fpdc. (42)

**Rnds 14-27:** Repeat Rnds 12-13.

**Rnd 28:** Ch2, 2fpdc in next stitch, fpdc19, 2fpdc in next stitch, hdc1, Motif 1, sl st in first fpdc. (44)

**Rnd 29:** Ch2, fpdc1, 2fpdc in next stitch, fpdc19, 2fpdc in next stitch, fpdc1, hdc1, Motif 2, sl st in first fpdc. (46)

**Rnd 30:** Ch2, fpdc2, 2fpdc in next stitch, fpdc19, 2fpdc in next stitch, fpdc2, hdc1, Motif 1, sl st in first fpdc. (48)

**Rnd 31:** Ch2, fpdc3, 2fpdc in next stitch, fpdc19, 2fpdc in next stitch, fpdc3, hdc1, Motif 2, sl st in first fpdc. (50)

**Rnd 32:** Ch2, fpdc4, 2fpdc in next stitch, fpdc19, 2fpdc in next stitch, fpdc4, hdc1, Motif 1, sl st in first fpdc. (52)

**Rnd 33:** Ch2, fpdc5, 2fpdc in next stitch, fpdc19, 2fpdc in next stitch, fpdc5, hdc1, Motif 2, sl st in first fpdc. (54)

**Rnd 34:** Ch2, fpdc5, fpdc2tog, fpdc19, fpdc2tog, fpdc5, hdc1, Motif 1, sl st in first fpdc. (52)

**Rnd 35:** Ch2, fpdc4, fpdc2tog, fpdc19, fpdc2tog, fpdc4, hdc1, Motif 2, sl st in first fpdc. (50)

**Rnd 36:** Ch2, fpdc3, fpdc2tog, fpdc19, fpdc2tog, fpdc3, hdc1, Motif 1, sl st in first fpdc. (48)

**Rnd 37:** Ch2, fpdc2, fpdc2tog, fpdc19, fpdc2tog, fpdc2, hdc1, Motif 2, sl st in first fpdc. (46)

**Rnd 38:** Ch2, fpdc1, fpdc2tog, fpdc19, fpdc2tog, fpdc1, hdc1, Motif 1, sl st in first fpdc. (44)

**Rnd 39:** Ch2, fpdc2tog, fpdc19, fpdc2tog, hdc1, Motif 2, sl st in first fpdc. (42)

**Rnd 40:** Ch2, bpdc1, Motif 1, hdc1, Motif 1, sl st in first bpdc. (42)

**Rnd 41:** Ch2, bpdc1, Motif 2, hdc1, Motif 2, sl st in first bpdc. (42)

**Rnds 42-45:** Repeat Rnds 40-41.

**Rnd 46:** Ch2, bpdc1, fpdc1 in each stitch to the hdc, hdc1, fpdc1 in each stitch to end, sl st in first bpdc. (42)

**Rnds 47-48:** Ch2, *bpdc1, fpdc1*, repeat * to * around, sl st in first bpdc. (42)

Fasten off and weave in ends.

Coffee bean small motif

**SIZE: SMALL**

---

**MOTIF 1:** Fpdc1, fpdc2tog, *3fpdc in next st, fpdc3tog*, repeat * to * to last 4 stitches, 3fpdc in next st, fpdc2tog, fpdc1.

**MOTIF 2:** Fpdc1, 2fpdc in next stitch, *fpdc3tog, 3fpdc in next st*, repeat * to * to last 5 stitches, fpdc3tog, 2fpdc in next stitch, fpdc1.

**Rnd 1:** Start with a magic loop, ch2 (first ch2 doesn't count as first dc throughout), 6dc in the loop, sl st in first dc. (6)

**Rnd 2:** Ch2, 2fpdc in each stitch around, sl st in first fpdc. (12)

**Rnd 3:** Ch2, *fpdc1, 2fpdc in next stitch*, repeat * to * 2 more times, hdc1, 2fpdc in next stitch, repeat * to * 2 more times, sl st in first fpdc. (18)

**Rnd 4:** Ch2, *fpdc2, 2fpdc in next stitch*, repeat * to * 2 more times, hdc1, fpdc1, 2fpdc in next stitch, repeat * to * 2 more times, sl st in first fpdc. (24)

**Rnd 5:** Ch2, *fpdc3, 2fpdc in next stitch*, repeat * to * 2 more times, hdc1, fpdc2, 2fpdc in next stitch, repeat * to * 2 more times, sl st in first fpdc. (30)

**Rnd 6:** Ch2, *fpdc4, 2fpdc in next stitch*, repeat * to * 2 more times, hdc1, fpdc3, 2fpdc in next stitch, repeat * to * 2 more times, sl st in first fpdc. (36)

**Rnd 7:** Ch2, *fpdc5, 2fpdc in next stitch*, repeat * to * 2 more times, hdc1, fpdc4, 2fpdc in next stitch, repeat * to * 2 more times, sl st in first fpdc. (42)

**Rnd 8:** Ch2, *fpdc6, 2fpdc in next stitch*, repeat * to * 2 more times, hdc1, fpdc5, 2fpdc in next stitch, repeat * to * 2 more times, sl st in first fpdc. (48)

**Rnds 9-13:** Ch2, fpdc24, hdc1, fpdc23, sl st in first fpdc. (48)

**Rnd 14:** Ch2, fpdc24, hdc1, Motif 1, sl st in first fpdc. (48)

**Rnd 15:** Ch2, fpdc24, hdc1, Motif 2, sl st in first fpdc. (48)

**Rnds 16-32:** Repeat Rnds 14-15; you'll end with Rnd 14.

**Rnd 33:** Ch2, 2fpdc in next stitch, fpdc22, 2fpdc in next stitch, hdc1, Motif 2, sl st in first fpdc. (50)

**Rnd 34:** Ch2, fpdc1, 2fpdc in next stitch, fpdc22, 2fpdc in next stitch, fpdc1, hdc1, Motif 1, sl st in first fpdc. (52)

**Rnd 35:** Ch2, fpdc2, 2fpdc in next stitch, fpdc22, 2fpdc in next stitch, fpdc2, hdc1, Motif 2, sl st in first fpdc. (54)

**Rnd 36:** Ch2, fpdc3, 2fpdc in next stitch, fpdc22, 2fpdc in next stitch, fpdc3, hdc1, Motif 1, sl st in first fpdc. (56)

**Rnd 37:** Ch2, fpdc4, 2fpdc in next stitch, fpdc22, 2fpdc in next stitch, fpdc4, hdc1, Motif 2, sl st in first fpdc. (58)

**Rnd 38:** Ch2, fpdc5, 2fpdc in next stitch, fpdc22, 2fpdc in next stitch, fpdc5, hdc1, Motif 1, sl st in first fpdc. (60)

**Rnd 39:** Ch2, fpdc6, 2fpdc in next stitch, fpdc22, 2fpdc in next stitch, fpdc6, hdc1, Motif 2, sl st in first fpdc. (62)

**Rnd 40:** Ch2, fpdc6, fpdc2tog, fpdc22, fpdc2tog, fpdc6, hdc1, Motif 1, sl st in first fpdc. (60)

2

1

Rnd 41: Ch2, fpdc5, fpdc2tog, fpdc22, fpdc2tog,
fpdc5, hdc1, Motif 2, sl st in first fpdc. (58)

Rnd 42: Ch2, fpdc4, fpdc2tog, fpdc22, fpdc2tog,
fpdc4, hdc1, Motif 1, sl st in first fpdc.
(56)

Rnd 43: Ch2, fpdc3, fpdc2tog, fpdc22, fpdc2tog,
fpdc3, hdc1, Motif 2, sl st in first fpdc.
(54)

Rnd 44: Ch2, fpdc2, fpdc2tog, fpdc22, fpdc2tog,
fpdc2, hdc1, Motif 1, sl st in first fpdc.
(52)

Rnd 45: Ch2, fpdc1, fpdc2tog, fpdc22, fpdc2tog,
fpdc1, hdc1, Motif 2, sl st in first fpdc.
(50)

Rnd 46: Ch2, fpdc2tog, fpdc22, fpdc2tog, hdc1,
Motif 1, sl st in first fpdc. (48)

Rnd 47: Ch2, bpdc1, Motif 2, hdc1, Motif 2, sl st in
first bpdc. (48)

Rnd 48: Ch2, bpdc1, Motif 1, hdc1, Motif 1, sl st in
first bpdc. (48)

Rnds 49-52: Repeat Rnds 47-48.

Rnd 53: Ch2, bpdc1, fpdc1 in each stitch to the hdc,
hdc1, fpdc1 in each stitch to end, sl st in
first bpdc. (48)

Rnds 54-55: Ch2, *bpdc1, fpdc1*, repeat * to *
around, sl st in first bpdc. (48)

Fasten off and weave in ends.

SIZE: MEDIUM

MOTIF 1: Fpdc2tog, *3fpdc in next st, fpdc3tog*,
repeat * to * to last 4 stitches, 3fpdc in next st,
fpdc2tog, fpdc1.

MOTIF 2: 2fpdc in next stitch, *fpdc3tog, 3fpdc
in next st*, repeat * to * to last 5 stitches,
fpdc3tog, 2fpdc in next stitch, fpdc1.

Rnd 1: Start with a magic loop, ch2 (first ch2
doesn't count as first dc throughout), 6dc in
the loop, sl st in first dc. (6)

Rnd 2: Ch2, 2fpdc in each stitch around, sl st in
first fpdc. (12)

Rnd 3: Ch2, *fpdc1, 2fpdc in next stitch*, repeat
* to * 2 more times, hdc1, 2fpdc in next
stitch, repeat * to * 2 more times, sl st in
first fpdc. (18)

Rnd 4: Ch2, *fpdc2, 2fpdc in next stitch*, repeat
* to * 2 more times, hdc1, fpdc1, 2fpdc in
next stitch, repeat * to * 2 more times, sl
st in first fpdc. (24)

Rnd 5: Ch2, *fpdc3, 2fpdc in next stitch*, repeat
* to * 2 more times, hdc1, fpdc2, 2fpdc in
next stitch, repeat * to * 2 more times, sl
st in first fpdc. (30)

Rnd 6: Ch2, *fpdc4, 2fpdc in next stitch*, repeat
* to * 2 more times, hdc1, fpdc3, 2fpdc in
next stitch, repeat * to * 2 more times, sl
st in first fpdc. (36)

Rnd 7: Ch2, *fpdc5, 2fpdc in next stitch*, repeat
* to * 2 more times, hdc1, fpdc4, 2fpdc in
next stitch, repeat * to * 2 more times, sl
st in first fpdc. (42)

**Rnd 8:** Ch2, *fpdc6, 2fpdc in next stitch*, repeat
* to * 2 more times, hdc1, fpdc5, 2fpdc in
next stitch, repeat * to * 2 more times, sl
st in first fpdc. (48)

**Rnd 9:** Ch2, *fpdc7, 2fpdc in next stitch*, repeat
* to * 2 more times, hdc1, fpdc6, 2fpdc in
next stitch, repeat * to * 2 more times, sl
st in first fpdc. (54)

**Rnds 10-15:** Ch2, fpdc27, hdc1, fpdc26, sl st in first
fpdc. (54)

**Rnd 16:** Ch2, fpdc27, hdc1, Motif 1, sl st in first
fpdc. (54)

**Rnd 17:** Ch2, fpdc27, hdc1, Motif 2, sl st in first
fpdc. (54)

**Rnds 18-37:** Repeat Rnds 16-17.

**Rnd 38:** Ch2, 2fpdc in next stitch, fpdc25, 2fpdc in
next stitch, hdc1, Motif 1, sl st in first
fpdc. (56)

**Rnd 39:** Ch2, fpdc1, 2fpdc in next stitch, fpdc25,
2fpdc in next stitch, fpdc1, hdc1, Motif 2,
sl st in first fpdc. (58)

**Rnd 40:** Ch2, fpdc2, 2fpdc in next stitch, fpdc25,
2fpdc in next stitch, fpdc2, hdc1, Motif 1,
sl st in first fpdc. (60)

**Rnd 41:** Ch2, fpdc3, 2fpdc in next stitch, fpdc25,
2fpdc in next stitch, fpdc3, hdc1, Motif 2,
sl st in first fpdc. (62)

**Rnd 42:** Ch2, fpdc4, 2fpdc in next stitch, fpdc25,
2fpdc in next stitch, fpdc4, hdc1, Motif 1,
sl st in first fpdc. (64)

**Rnd 43:** Ch2, fpdc5, 2fpdc in next stitch, fpdc25,
2fpdc in next stitch, fpdc5, hdc1, Motif 2,
sl st in first fpdc. (66)

**Rnd 44:** Ch2, fpdc6, 2fpdc in next stitch, fpdc25,
2fpdc in next stitch, fpdc6, hdc1, Motif 1,
sl st in first fpdc. (68)

**Rnd 45:** Ch2, fpdc7, 2fpdc in next stitch, fpdc25,
2fpdc in next stitch, fpdc7, hdc1, Motif 2,
sl st in first fpdc. (70)

**Rnd 46:** Ch2, fpdc7, fpdc2tog, fpdc25, fpdc2tog,
fpdc7, hdc1, Motif 1, sl st in first fpdc.
(68)

**Rnd 47:** Ch2, fpdc6, fpdc2tog, fpdc25, fpdc2tog,
fpdc6, hdc1, Motif 2, sl st in first fpdc.
(66)

**Rnd 48:** Ch2, fpdc5, fpdc2tog, fpdc25, fpdc2tog,
fpdc5, hdc1, Motif 1, sl st in first fpdc.
(64)

**Rnd 49:** Ch2, fpdc4, fpdc2tog, fpdc25, fpdc2tog,
fpdc4, hdc1, Motif 2, sl st in first fpdc.
(62)

**Rnd 50:** Ch2, fpdc3, fpdc2tog, fpdc25, fpdc2tog,
fpdc3, hdc1, Motif 1, sl st in first fpdc.
(60)

**Rnd 51:** Ch2, fpdc2, fpdc2tog, fpdc25, fpdc2tog,
fpdc2, hdc1, Motif 2, sl st in first fpdc.
(58)

**Rnd 52:** Ch2, fpdc1, fpdc2tog, fpdc25, fpdc2tog,
fpdc1, hdc1, Motif 1, sl st in first fpdc.
(56)

**Rnd 53:** Ch2, fpdc2tog, fpdc25, fpdc2tog, hdc1,
Motif 2, sl st in first fpdc. (54)

**Rnd 54:** Ch2, bpdc1, Motif 1, hdc1, Motif 1, sl st in
first bpdc. (54)

**Rnd 55:** Ch2, bpdc1, Motif 2, hdc1, Motif 2, sl st in
first bpdc. (54)

**Rnds 56-61:** Repeat Rnds 54-55.

**Rnd 62:** Ch2, bpdc1, fpdc1 in each stitch to the hdc,
hdc1, fpdc1 in each stitch to end, sl st in
first bpdc. (54)

**Rnds 63-64:** Ch2, *bpdc1, fpdc1*, repeat * to *
around, sl st in first bpdc. (54)

Fasten off and weave in ends.

# little bear

**NOTE**
The socks as described in the pattern are for the bear version. For the panda, replace the light blue with black, and the white and beige with light gray. Finish the cuff with black, as shown.

THE CUTE FACES OF THESE BEARS APPEAL TO EVERYONE!
THIS CUDDLY VARIETY IS A FAVORITE FOR BIG AND SMALL.

For help in choosing the right size, see page 15.
For help in choosing the right hook size and checking gauge, see page 16.

## CHANGING COLORS

The best way to change colors is to complete the last step of the stitch before the color change with the new color. For these socks that means: When making the last fpdc before the color change, use the new color for the last yarn over and pull through (so the sl st doesn't count as the last stitch). In between the color changes, you don't have to cut the color you're not using. You can simply pick it up again when needed, but make sure the loops of yarn are loose enough to stretch a bit.

## MATERIALS

**Yarn**
**Bear Version (light blue, white, and beige):**
Durable Soqs, #1 super fine weight (75% wool, 25% polyamide; 230 yd./210 m per 1.76 oz./50 g); colors #289, #326, and #422

**Panda Version (black and light gray):**
Sheepjes Metropolis, #1 super fine weight (75% wool, 25% nylon; 218.7 yd./200 m per 1.75 oz./50 g); colors #080 and #025

**Hook**
US size G-6 (4 mm)

**Gauge**
5 fpdc wide and 4 rnds high = 0.7 in./2 cm

**Estimated total yarn required**
0–6 months: 230 yd./210 m; 12–24 months: 230 yd./210 m; 3–5 years: 460 yd./420 m; 6–10 years: 460 yd./420 m; Small: 460 yd./420 m; Medium: 689 yd./630 m

## ABBREVIATIONS

| | | |
|---|---|---|
| ⟲ | **ch** | chain |
| ⊤ | **dc** | double crochet |
| ⌠ | **fpdc** | front post double crochet |
| ⌡ | **bpdc** | back post double crochet |
| ● | **sl st** | slip stitch |
| Ⱥ | **fpdc2tog** | front post double crochet 2 together (1 stitch decreased) |
| ⱴ | **2 fpdc in the next stitch** | 2 fpdc in the same stitch (1 stitch increased) |

## EYES

### SIZE 0-6 MONTHS AND 12-24 MONTHS

**Rnd 1:** With black, start with a magic loop, ch2, 4sc in the loop, sl st in first sc. Cut a long thread to attach the eye with in Rnd 21 (0-6 months) or Rnd 30 (12-24 months) right beneath the ears. Add a little white accent to make the eyes pop.

### SIZE 3-5 YEARS TO MEDIUM

**Rnd 1:** With black, start with a magic loop, ch2, 6sc in the loop, sl st in first sc. Cut a long thread to attach the eye with in Rnd 39 (3-5 years), Rnd 48 (6-10 years), Rnd 57 (Small), or Rnd 66 (Medium) right beneath the ears. Add a little white accent to make the eyes pop.

## MUZZLE

Embroider the nose and mouth centered in between the eyes across 3 stitches.

## SIZE: 0-6 MONTHS

**Rnd 1:** **With light blue,** start with a magic loop, ch2 (first ch2 doesn't count as first dc throughout the pattern), 6dc in the loop, sl st in first dc. (6)

**Rnd 2:** Ch2, 2fpdc in each stitch around, sl st in first fpdc. (12)

**Rnd 3:** Ch2, *fpdc1, 2fpdc in next stitch*, repeat * to * 2 more times, hdc1, 2fpdc in next stitch, repeat * to * 2 more times, sl st in first fpdc. (18)

**Rnd 4:** Ch2, *fpdc2, 2fpdc in next stitch*, repeat * to * 2 more times, hdc1, fpdc1, 2fpdc in next stitch, repeat * to * 2 more times, sl st in first fpdc. (24)

**Rnds 5-8:** Ch2, fpdc12, hdc1, fpdc11, sl st in first fpdc. (24)

**Rnd 9:** **With white,** ch2, fpdc12, hdc1, fpdc11, sl st in first fpdc. (24)

**Rnd 10:** **With light blue,** ch2, fpdc12, hdc1, fpdc11, sl st in first fpdc. (24)

**Rnd 11:** **With white,** ch2, fpdc12, hdc1, fpdc11, sl st in first fpdc. (24)

**Rnd 12:** **With light blue,** ch2, fpdc12, hdc1, fpdc11, sl st in first fpdc. (24)

**Rnd 13:** **With white,** ch2, 2fpdc in next stitch, fpdc10, 2fpdc in next stitch, hdc1, fpdc11, sl st in first fpdc. (26)

**Rnd 14:** **With light blue,** ch2, fpdc1, 2fpdc in next stitch, fpdc10, 2fpdc in next stitch, fpdc1, hdc1, fpdc11, sl st in first fpdc. (28)

**Rnd 15:** **With white,** ch2, fpdc2, 2fpdc in next stitch, fpdc10, 2fpdc in next stitch, fpdc2, hdc1, fpdc11, sl st in first fpdc. (30)

**Rnd 16:** **With beige (you can cut the white and blue yarn),** ch2, fpdc2, fpdc2tog, fpdc10, fpdc2tog, fpdc2, hdc1, fpdc11, sl st in first fpdc. (28)

**Rnd 17:** Ch2, fpdc1, fpdc2tog, fpdc10, fpdc2tog, fpdc1, hdc1, fpdc11, sl st in first fpdc. (26)

**Rnd 18:** Ch2, fpdc2tog, fpdc10, fpdc2tog, hdc1, fpdc11, sl st in first fpdc. (24)

**Rnds 19-21:** Ch2, fpdc12, hdc1, fpdc11, sl st in first fpdc. (24)

**Rnds 22-23:** Ch2, *fpdc1, bpdc1*, repeat * to * around, sl st in first fpdc. (24)

**Rnd 24:** Ch2, *fpdc1, bpdc1*, repeat * to * over 14 stitches, 6fpdc in next stitch, bpdc1, repeat from * to * over the next 4 stitches, 6fpdc in next stitch, bpdc1, fpdc1, bpdc1, sl st in first fpdc. (24)

Fasten off and weave in ends.

## SIZE: 12-24 MONTHS

**Rnd 1:** **With light blue,** start with a magic loop, ch2 (first ch2 doesn't count as first dc throughout the pattern), 6dc in the loop, sl st in first dc. (6)

**Rnd 2:** Ch2, 2fpdc in each stitch around, sl st in first fpdc. (12)

**Rnd 3:** Ch2, *fpdc1, 2fpdc in next st*, repeat * to * 2 more times, hdc1, 2fpdc in next st, repeat * to * 2 more times, sl st in first fpdc. (18)

**Rnd 4:** Ch2, *fpdc2, 2fpdc in next st*, repeat * to * 2 more times, hdc1, fpdc1, 2fpdc in next st, repeat * to * 2 more times, sl st in first fpdc. (24)

**Rnd 5:** Ch2, *fpdc3, 2fpdc in next st*, repeat * to * 2 more times, hdc1, fpdc2, 2fpdc in next st, repeat * to * 2 more times, sl st in first fpdc. (30)

**Rnds 6-10:** Ch2, fpdc15, hdc1, fpdc14, sl st in first fpdc. (30)

**Rnds 11-12:** **With white,** ch2, fpdc15, hdc1, fpdc14, sl st in first fpdc. (30)

**Rnds 13-14:** **With light blue,** ch2, fpdc15, hdc1, fpdc14, sl st in first fpdc. (30)

**Rnds 15–16:** **With white,** ch2, fpdc15, hdc1, fpdc14, sl st in first fpdc. (30)

**Rnd 17:** **With light blue,** ch2, fpdc15, hdc1, fpdc14, sl st in first fpdc. (30)

**Rnd 18:** Ch2, 2fpdc in next st, fpdc13, 2fpdc in next st, hdc1, fpdc14, sl st in first fpdc (32)

**Rnd 19:** **With white,** ch2, fpdc1, 2fpdc in next st, fpdc13, 2fpdc in next st, fpdc1, hdc1, fpdc14, sl st in first fpdc. (34)

**Rnd 20:** Ch2, fpdc2, 2fpdc in next st, fpdc13, 2fpdc in next st, fpdc2, hdc1, fpdc14, sl st in first fpdc. (36)

**Rnd 21:** **With light blue,** ch2, fpdc3, 2fpdc in next st, fpdc13, 2fpdc in next st, fpdc3, hdc1, fpdc14, sl st in first fpdc. (38)

**Rnd 22:** Ch2, fpdc3, fpdc2tog, fpdc13, fpdc2tog, fpdc3, hdc1, fpdc14, sl st in first fpdc. (36)

**Rnd 23:** **With white,** ch2, fpdc2, fpdc2tog, fpdc13, fpdc2tog, fpdc2, hdc1, fpdc14, sl st in first fpdc. (34)

**Rnd 24:** Ch2, fpdc1, fpdc2tog, fpdc13, fpdc2tog, fpdc1, hdc1, fpdc14, sl st in first fpdc. (32)

**Rnd 25:** **With beige (you can cut the white and blue yarn),** ch2, fpdc2tog, fpdc13, fpdc2tog, hdc1, fpdc14, sl st in first fpdc. (30)

**Rnds 26–30:** Ch2, fpdc15, hdc1, fpdc14, sl st in first fpdc. (30)

**Rnds 31–33:** Ch2, *fpdc1, bpdc1*, repeat * to * around, sl st in first fpdc. (30)

**Rnd 34:** Ch2, *fpdc1, bpdc1*, repeat * to * over 18 stitches, 6fpdc in next stitch, bpdc1, repeat from * to * over the next 6 stitches, 6fpdc in next stitch, bpdc1, fpdc1, bpdc1, sl st in first fpdc. (30)

Fasten off and weave in ends.

**SIZE: 3–5 YEARS**

**Rnd 1:** **With light blue,** start with a magic loop, ch2 (first ch2 doesn't count as first dc throughout the pattern), 6dc in the loop, sl st in first dc. (6)

**Rnd 2:** Ch2, 2fpdc in each stitch around, sl st in first fpdc. (12)

**Rnd 3:** Ch2, *fpdc1, 2fpdc in next st*, repeat * to * 2 more times, hdc1, 2fpdc in next st, repeat * to * 2 more times, sl st in first fpdc. (18)

**Rnd 4:** Ch2, *fpdc2, 2fpdc in next st*, repeat * to * 2 more times, hdc1, fpdc1, 2fpdc in next st, repeat * to * 2 more times, sl st in first fpdc. (24)

**Rnd 5:** Ch2, *fpdc3, 2fpdc in next st*, repeat * to * 2 more times, hdc1, fpdc2, 2fpdc in next st, repeat * to * 2 more times, sl st in first fpdc. (30)

**Rnd 6:** Ch2, *fpdc4, 2fpdc in next st*, repeat * to * 2 more times, hdc1, fpdc3, 2fpdc in next st, repeat * to * 2 more times, sl st in first fpdc. (36)

**Rnds 7–12:** Ch2, fpdc18, hdc1, fpdc17, sl st in first fpdc. (36)

**Rnds 13–15:** **With white,** ch2, fpdc18, hdc1, fpdc17, sl st in first fpdc. (36)

**Rnds 16–18:** **With light blue,** ch2, fpdc18, hdc1, fpdc17, sl st in first fpdc. (36)

**Rnds 19–21:** **With white,** ch2, fpdc18, hdc1, fpdc17, sl st in first fpdc. (36)

**Rnd 22:** **With light blue,** ch2, fpdc18, hdc1, fpdc17, sl st in first fpdc. (36)

**Rnd 23:** Ch2, 2fpdc in next st, fpdc16, 2fpdc in next st, hdc1, fpdc17, sl st in first fpdc. (38)

**Rnd 24:** Ch2, fpdc1, 2fpdc in next st, fpdc16, 2fpdc in next st, fpdc1, hdc1, fpdc17, sl st in first fpdc. (40)

**Rnd 25:** **With white,** ch2, fpdc2, 2fpdc in next st, fpdc16, 2fpdc in next st, fpdc2, hdc1, fpdc17, sl st in first fpdc. (42)

**Rnd 26:** Ch2, fpdc3, 2fpdc in next st, fpdc16, 2fpdc in next st, fpdc3, hdc1, fpdc17, sl st in first fpdc. (44)

**Rnd 27:** Ch2, fpdc4, 2fpdc in next st, fpdc16, 2fpdc in next st, fpdc4, hdc1, fpdc17, sl st in first fpdc. (46)

**Rnd 28:** **With light blue,** ch2, fpdc4, fpdc2tog, fpdc16, fpdc2tog, fpdc4, hdc1, fpdc17, sl st in first fpdc. (44)

**Rnd 29:** Ch2, fpdc3, fpdc2tog, fpdc16, fpdc2tog, fpdc3, hdc1, fpdc17, sl st in first fpdc. (42)

**Rnd 30:** Ch2, fpdc2, fpdc2tog, fpdc16, fpdc2tog, fpdc2, hdc1, fpdc17, sl st in first fpdc. (40)

**Rnd 31:** **With white,** ch2, fpdc1, fpdc2tog, fpdc16, fpdc2tog, fpdc1, hdc1, fpdc17, sl st in first fpdc. (38)

**Rnd 32:** Ch2, fpdc2tog, fpdc16, fpdc2tog, hdc1, fpdc17, sl st in first fpdc. (36)

**Rnd 33:** Ch2, fpdc18, hdc1, fpdc17, sl st in first fpdc. (36)

**Rnd 34:** **With beige (you can cut the white and blue yarn),** ch2, fpdc18, hdc1, fpdc17, sl st in first fpdc. (36)

**Rnds 35-39:** Ch2, fpdc18, hdc1, fpdc17, sl st in first fpdc. (36)

**Rnds 40-43:** Ch2, *fpdc1, bpdc1*, repeat * to * around, sl st in first fpdc. (36)

**Rnd 44:** Ch2, *fpdc1, bpdc1*, repeat * to * over 22 stitches, 6fpdc in next stitch, bpdc1, repeat from * to * over the next 6 stitches, 6fpdc in next stitch, bpdc1, repeat from * to * over the next 4 stitches, sl st in first fpdc. (36)

Fasten off and weave in ends.

## SIZE: 6-10 YEARS

**Rnd 1:** **With light blue,** start with a magic loop, ch2 (first ch2 doesn't count as first dc throughout the pattern), 6dc in the loop, sl st in first dc. (6)

**Rnd 2:** Ch2, 2fpdc in each stitch around, sl st in first fpdc. (12)

**Rnd 3:** Ch2, *fpdc1, 2fpdc in next st*, repeat * to * 2 more times, hdc1, 2fpdc in next st, repeat * to * 2 more times, sl st in first fpdc. (18)

**Rnd 4:** Ch2, *fpdc2, 2fpdc in next st*, repeat * to * 2 more times, hdc1, fpdc1, 2fpdc in next st, repeat * to * 2 more times, sl st in first fpdc. (24)

**Rnd 5:** Ch2, *fpdc3, 2fpdc in next st*, repeat * to * 2 more times, hdc1, fpdc2, 2fpdc in next st, repeat * to * 2 more times, sl st in first fpdc. (30)

**Rnd 6:** Ch2, *fpdc4, 2fpdc in next st*, repeat * to * 2 more times, hdc1, fpdc3, 2fpdc in next st, repeat * to * 2 more times, sl st in first fpdc. (36)

**Rnd 7:** Ch2, *fpdc5, 2fpdc in next st*, repeat * to * 2 more times, hdc1, fpdc4, 2fpdc in next st, repeat * to * 2 more times, sl st in first fpdc. (42)

**Rnds 8-14:** Ch2, fpdc21, hdc1, fpdc20, sl st in first fpdc. (42)

**Rnds 15-18:** **With white,** ch2, fpdc21, hdc1, fpdc20, sl st in first fpdc. (42)

**Rnds 19-22:** **With light blue,** ch2, fpdc21, hdc1, fpdc20, sl st in first fpdc. (42)

**Rnds 23-26:** **With white,** ch2, fpdc21, hdc1, fpdc20, sl st in first fpdc. (42)

**Rnd 27:** **With light blue,** ch2, fpdc21, hdc1, fpdc20, sl st in first fpdc. (42)

**Rnd 28:** Ch2, 2fpdc in next st, fpdc19, 2fpdc in next st, hdc1, fpdc20, sl st in first fpdc. (44)

**Rnd 29:** Ch2, fpdc1, 2fpdc in next st, fpdc19, 2fpdc in next st, fpdc1, hdc1, fpdc20, sl st in first fpdc. (46)

**Rnd 30:** Ch2, fpdc2, 2fpdc in next st, fpdc19, 2fpdc in next st, fpdc2, hdc1, fpdc20, sl st in first fpdc. (48)

**Rnd 31:** **With white,** ch2, fpdc3, 2fpdc in next st, fpdc19, 2fpdc in next st, fpdc3, hdc1, fpdc20, sl st in first fpdc. (50)

**Rnd 32:** Ch2, fpdc4, 2fpdc in next st, fpdc19, 2fpdc in next st, fpdc4, hdc1, fpdc20, sl st in first fpdc. (52)

**Rnd 33:** Ch2, fpdc5, 2fpdc in next st, fpdc19, 2fpdc in next st, fpdc5, hdc1, fpdc20, sl st in first fpdc. (54)

**Rnd 34:** Ch2, fpdc5, fpdc2tog, fpdc19, fpdc2tog, fpdc5, hdc1, fpdc20, sl st in first fpdc. (52)

**Rnd 35:** **With light blue,** ch2, fpdc4, fpdc2tog, fpdc19, fpdc2tog, fpdc4, hdc1, fpdc20, sl st in first fpdc. (50)

**Rnd 36:** Ch2, fpdc3, fpdc2tog, fpdc19, fpdc2tog, fpdc3, hdc1, fpdc20, sl st in first fpdc. (48)

**Rnd 37:** Ch2, fpdc2, fpdc2tog, fpdc19, fpdc2tog, fpdc2, hdc1, fpdc20, sl st in first fpdc. (46)

**Rnd 38:** Ch2, fpdc1, fpdc2tog, fpdc19, fpdc2tog, fpdc1, hdc1, fpdc20, sl st in first fpdc. (44)

**Rnd 39:** **With white,** ch2, fpdc2tog, fpdc19, fpdc2tog, hdc1, fpdc20, sl st in first fpdc. (42)

**Rnds 40-42:** Ch2, fpdc21, hdc1, fpdc20, sl st in first fpdc. (42)

**Rnd 43:** **With beige (you can cut the white and blue yarn),** ch2, fpdc21, hdc1, fpdc20, sl st in first fpdc. (42)

**Rnds 44-48:** Ch2, fpdc21, hdc1, fpdc20, sl st in first fpdc. (42)

**Rnds 49-53:** Ch2, *fpdc1, bpdc1*, repeat * to * around, sl st in first fpdc. (42)

**Rnd 54:** Ch2, *fpdc1, bpdc1*, repeat * to * over 26 stitches, 6fpdc in next stitch, bpdc1, repeat from * to * over the next 6 stitches, 6fpdc in next stitch, bpdc1, repeat from * to * over the next 6 stitches, sl st in first fpdc. (42)

Fasten off and weave in ends.

SIZE: SMALL

**Rnd 1:** **With light blue,** start with a magic loop, ch2 (first ch2 doesn't count as first dc throughout the pattern), 6dc in the loop, sl st in first dc. (6)

**Rnd 2:** Ch2, 2fpdc in each stitch around, sl st in first fpdc. (12)

**Rnd 3:** Ch2, *fpdc1, 2fpdc in next st*, repeat * to * 2 more times, hdc1, 2fpdc in next st, repeat * to * 2 more times, sl st in first fpdc. (18)

**Rnd 4:** Ch2, *fpdc2, 2fpdc in next st*, repeat * to * 2 more times, hdc1, fpdc1, 2fpdc in next st, repeat * to * 2 more times, sl st in first fpdc. (24)

**Rnd 5:** Ch2, *fpdc3, 2fpdc in next st*, repeat * to * 2 more times, hdc1, fpdc2, 2fpdc in next st, repeat * to * 2 more times, sl st in first fpdc. (30)

**Rnd 6:** Ch2, *fpdc4, 2fpdc in next st*, repeat * to * 2 more times, hdc1, fpdc3, 2fpdc in next st, repeat * to * 2 more times, sl st in first fpdc. (36)

**Rnd 7:** Ch2, *fpdc5, 2fpdc in next st*, repeat * to * 2 more times, hdc1, fpdc4, 2fpdc in next st, repeat * to * 2 more times, sl st in first fpdc. (42)

**Rnd 8:** Ch2, *fpdc6, 2fpdc in next st*, repeat * to * 2 more times, hdc1, fpdc5, 2fpdc in next st, repeat * to * 2 more times, sl st in first fpdc. (48)

**Rnds 9-16:** Ch2, fpdc24, hdc1, fpdc23, sl st in first fpdc. (48)

**Rnds 17-21:** **With white,** ch2, fpdc24, hdc1, fpdc23, sl st in first fpdc. (48)

**Rnds 22-26:** **With light blue,** ch2, fpdc24, hdc1, fpdc23, sl st in first fpdc. (48)

**Rnds 27-31:** **With white,** ch2, fpdc24, hdc1, fpdc23, sl st in first fpdc. (48)

**Rnd 32:** **With light blue,** ch2, fpdc24, hdc1, fpdc23, sl st in first fpdc. (48)

**Rnd 33:** Ch2, 2fpdc in next st, fpdc22, 2fpdc in next st, hdc1, fpdc23, sl st in first fpdc. (50)

**Rnd 34:** Ch2, fpdc1, 2fpdc in next st, fpdc22, 2fpdc in next st, fpdc1, hdc1, fpdc23, sl st in first fpdc. (52)

**Rnd 35:** Ch2, fpdc2, 2fpdc in next st, fpdc22, 2fpdc in next st, fpdc2, hdc1, fpdc23, sl st in first fpdc. (54)

**Rnd 36:** Ch2, fpdc3, 2fpdc in next st, fpdc22, 2fpdc in next st, fpdc3, hdc1, fpdc23, sl st in first fpdc. (56)

**Rnd 37:** **With white,** ch2, fpdc4, 2fpdc in next st, fpdc22, 2fpdc in next st, fpdc4, hdc1, fpdc23, sl st in first fpdc. (58)

**Rnd 38:** Ch2, fpdc5, 2fpdc in next st, fpdc22, 2fpdc in next st, fpdc5, hdc1, fpdc23, sl st in first fpdc. (60)

**Rnd 39:** Ch2, fpdc6, 2fpdc in next st, fpdc22, 2fpdc in next st, fpdc6, hdc1, fpdc23, sl st in first fpdc. (62)

**Rnd 40:** Ch2, fpdc6, fpdc2tog, fpdc22, fpdc2tog, fpdc6, hdc1, fpdc23, sl st in first fpdc. (60)

**Rnd 41:** Ch2, fpdc5, fpdc2tog, fpdc22, fpdc2tog, fpdc5, hdc1, fpdc23, sl st in first fpdc. (58)

**Rnd 42:** **With light blue,** ch2, fpdc4, fpdc2tog, fpdc22, fpdc2to fpdc2tog, fpdc4, hdc1, fpdc23, sl st in first fpdc. (56)

**Rnd 43:** Ch2, fpdc3, fpdc2tog, fpdc22, fpdc2tog, fpdc3, hdc1, fpdc23, sl st in first fpdc. (54)

**Rnd 44:** Ch2, fpdc2, fpdc2tog, fpdc22, fpdc2tog, fpdc2, hdc1, fpdc23, sl st in first fpdc. (52)

**Rnd 45:** Ch2, fpdc1, fpdc2tog, fpdc22, fpdc2tog, fpdc1, hdc1, fpdc23, sl st in first fpdc. (50)

**Rnd 46:** Ch2, fpdc2tog, fpdc22, fpdc2tog, hdc1, fpdc23, sl st in first fpdc. (48)

**Rnd 47:** **With white,** ch2, fpdc24, hdc1, fpdc23, sl st in first fpdc. (48)

**Rnds 48-51:** Ch2, fpdc24, hdc1, fpdc23, sl st in first fpdc. (48)

**Rnd 52:** **With beige (you can cut the white and blue yarn),** ch2, fpdc24, hdc1, fpdc23, sl st in first fpdc. (48)

**Rnds 53-57:** Ch2, fpdc24, hdc1, fpdc23, sl st in first fpdc. (48)

**Rnds 58-63:** Ch2, *fpdc1, bpdc1*, repeat * to * around, sl st in first fpdc. (48)

**Rnd 64:** Ch2, *fpdc1, bpdc1*, repeat * to * over 30 stitches, 6fpdc in next stitch, bpdc1, repeat from * to * over the next 6 stitches, 6fpdc in next stitch, bpdc1, repeat from * to * over the next 8 stitches, sl st in first fpdc. (48)

Fasten off and weave in ends.

**Rnd 1:** **With light blue,** start with a magic loop, ch2 (first ch2 doesn't count as first dc throughout the pattern), 6dc in the loop, sl st in first dc. (6)

**Rnd 2:** Ch2, 2fpdc in each stitch around, sl st in first fpdc. (12)

**Rnd 3:** Ch2, *fpdc1, 2fpdc in next st*, repeat * to * 2 more times, hdc1, 2fpdc in next st, repeat * to * 2 more times, sl st in first fpdc. (18)

**Rnd 4:** Ch2, *fpdc2, 2fpdc in next st*, repeat * to * 2 more times, hdc1, fpdc1, 2fpdc in next st, repeat * to * 2 more times, sl st in first fpdc. (24)

**Rnd 5:** Ch2, *fpdc3, 2fpdc in next st*, repeat * to * 2 more times, hdc1, fpdc2, 2fpdc in next st, repeat * to * 2 more times, sl st in first fpdc. (30)

**Rnd 6:** Ch2, *fpdc4, 2fpdc in next st*, repeat * to * 2 more times, hdc1, fpdc3, 2fpdc in next st, repeat * to * 2 more times, sl st in first fpdc. (36)

**Rnd 7:** Ch2, *fpdc5, 2fpdc in next st*, repeat * to * 2 more times, hdc1, fpdc4, 2fpdc in next st, repeat * to * 2 more times, sl st in first fpdc. (42)

**Rnd 8:** Ch2, *fpdc6, 2fpdc in next st*, repeat * to * 2 more times, hdc1, fpdc5, 2fpdc in next st, repeat * to * 2 more times, sl st in first fpdc. (48)

**Rnd 9:** Ch2, *fpdc7, 2fpdc in next st*, repeat * to * 2 more times, hdc1, fpdc6, 2fpdc in next st, repeat * to * 2 more times, sl st in first fpdc. (54)

**Rnds 10–18:** Ch2, fpdc27, hdc1, fpdc26, sl st in first fpdc. (54)

**Rnds 19–24:** **With white,** ch2, fpdc27, hdc1, fpdc26, sl st in first fpdc. (54)

**Rnds 25–30:** **With light blue,** ch2, fpdc27, hdc1, fpdc26, sl st in first fpdc. (54)

**Rnds 31–36:** **With white,** ch2, fpdc27, hdc1, fpdc26, sl st in first fpdc. (54)

**Rnd 37:** **With light blue,** Ch2, fpdc27, hdc1, fpdc26, sl st in first fpdc. (54)

**Rnd 38:** Ch2, 2fpdc in next st, fpdc25, 2fpdc in next st, hdc1, fpdc26, sl st in first fpdc. (56)

**Rnd 39:** Ch2, fpdc1, 2fpdc in next st, fpdc25, 2fpdc in next st, fpdc1, hdc1, fpdc26, sl st in first fpdc. (58)

**Rnd 40:** Ch2, fpdc2, 2fpdc in next st, fpdc25, 2fpdc in next st, fpdc2, hdc1, fpdc26, sl st in first fpdc. (60)

**Rnd 41:** Ch2, fpdc3, 2fpdc in next st, fpdc25, 2fpdc in next st, fpdc3, hdc1, fpdc26, sl st in first fpdc. (62)

**Rnd 42:** Ch2, fpdc4, 2fpdc in next st, fpdc25, 2fpdc in next st, fpdc4, hdc1, fpdc26, sl st in first fpdc. (64)

**Rnd 43:** **With white,** ch2, fpdc5, 2fpdc in next st, fpdc25, 2fpdc in next st, fpdc5, hdc1, fpdc26, sl st in first fpdc. (66)

**Rnd 44:** Ch2, fpdc6, 2fpdc in next st, fpdc25, 2fpdc in next st, fpdc6, hdc1, fpdc26, sl st in first fpdc. (68)

**Rnd 45:** Ch2, fpdc7, 2fpdc in next st, fpdc25, 2fpdc in next st, fpdc7, hdc1, fpdc26, sl st in first fpdc. (70)

**Rnd 46:** Ch2, fpdc7, fpdc2tog, fpdc25, fpdc2tog, fpdc7, hdc1, fpdc26, sl st in first fpdc. (68)

**Rnd 47:** Ch2, fpdc6, fpdc2tog, fpdc25, fpdc2tog, fpdc6, hdc1, fpdc26, sl st in first fpdc. (66)

**Rnd 48:** Ch2, fpdc5, fpdc2tog, fpdc25, fpdc2tog, fpdc5, hdc1, fpdc26, sl st in first fpdc. (64)

**Rnd 49:** **With light blue,** ch2, fpdc4, fpdc2tog, fpdc25, fpdc2tog, fpdc4, hdc1, fpdc26, sl st in first fpdc. (62)

**Rnd 50:** Ch2, fpdc3, fpdc2tog, fpdc25, fpdc2tog, fpdc3, hdc1, fpdc26, sl st in first fpdc. (60)

**Rnd 51:** Ch2, fpdc2, fpdc2tog, fpdc25, fpdc2tog, fpdc2, hdc1, fpdc26, sl st in first fpdc. (58)

**Rnd 52:** Ch2, fpdc1, fpdc2tog, fpdc25, fpdc2tog, fpdc1, hdc1, fpdc26, sl st in first fpdc. (56)

**Rnd 53:** Ch2, fpdc2tog, fpdc25, fpdc2tog, hdc1, fpdc26, sl st in first fpdc. (54)

**Rnd 54:** Ch2, fpdc27, hdc1, fpdc26, sl st in first fpdc. (54)

**Rnd 55:** **With white,** ch2, fpdc27, hdc1, fpdc26, sl st in first fpdc. (54)

**Rnds 56–60:** Ch2, fpdc27, hdc1, fpdc26, sl st in first fpdc. (54)

**Rnd 61:** **With beige (you can cut the white and blue yarn),** ch2, fpdc27, hdc1, fpdc26, sl st in first fpdc. (54)

**Rnds 62–66:** Ch2, fpdc27, hdc1, fpdc26, sl st in first fpdc. (54)

**Rnds 67–73:** Ch2, *fpdc1, bpdc1*, repeat * to * around, sl st in first fpdc. (54)

**Rnd 74:** Ch2, *fpdc1, bpdc1*, repeat * to * over 32 stitches, 6fpdc in next stitch, bpdc1, repeat from * to * over the next 8 stitches, 6fpdc in next stitch, bpdc1, repeat from * to * over the next 10 stitches, sl st in first fpdc. (54)

Fasten off and weave in ends.

# veiltail

**difficulty level:** 3 of 5

THE COMBINATION OF THE BEAUTIFUL CHEVRON PATTERN AND THE LOW
ANKLE MAKES THIS AN EYE-CATCHING AND QUICK SOCK OR BOOTY.
IT'S THE PERFECT LOUNGING SOCK FOR ADULTS AND KIDS.

For help in choosing the right size, see page 15.
For help in choosing the right hook size and checking gauge, see page 16.

## MATERIALS

### Yarn
**Turquoise socks:**
> Lana Grossa Meilenweit Soja Soft, #1 super fine
> weight (60% pure wool, 20% viscose, 20% poly-
> amide; 437.5 yd./400 m per 3.5 oz./100 g); color
> #304

**Multicolored socks:**
> Lana Grossa Glamy, #1 super fine weight (72%
> virgin wool, 26% polyamide, 2% polyester; 416
> yd./380 m per 3.5 oz./100 g); color #2705

### Hook
US size G-6 (4 mm)

### Gauge
5 fpdc wide and 4 rnds high = 0.7 in./2 cm

### Estimated total yarn required
0–6 months: 230 yd./210 m; 12–24 months: 230 yd./210 m; 3–5
years: 460 yd./420 m; 6–10 years: 460 yd./420 m; Small: 460
yd./420 m; Medium: 689 yd./630 m

## ABBREVIATIONS

| | | |
|---|---|---|
| ⌒ | **ch** | chain |
| ⊤ | **dc** | double crochet |
| ⌡ | **fpdc** | front post double crochet |
| ⌡ | **bpdc** | back post double crochet |
| ⌡ | **bphdc** | back post half double crochet |
| ● | **sl st** | slip stitch |
| ⊤ | **hdc** | half double crochet |
| ⋏ | **fpdc2tog** | front post double crochet 2 together (1 stitch decreased) |
| ⋎ | **2fpdc in next stitch** | 2 fpdc in the same stitch (1 stitch increased) |

**SIZE: 0–6 MONTHS**

---

**Chevron 0–6 months:** Bpdc1, 2 fpdc in next st, fpdc1, fpdc2tog, fpdc1, fpdc2tog, fpdc1, 2fpdc in next st, bpdc1.

**Rnd 1:** Start with a magic loop, ch2 (first ch2 doesn't count as first dc throughout the pattern), 6dc in the loop, sl st in first dc. (6)

**Rnd 2:** Ch2, 2fpdc in each stitch around, sl st in first fpdc. (12)

**Rnd 3:** Ch2, *fpdc1, 2fpdc in next st*, repeat * to * 2 more times, hdc1, 2fpdc in next st, repeat * to * 2 more times, sl st in first fpdc. (18)

**Rnd 4:** Ch2, *fpdc2, 2fpdc in next st*, repeat * to * 2 more times, hdc1, fpdc1, 2fpdc in next st, repeat * to * 2 more times, sl st in first fpdc. (24)

**Rnds 5–8:** Ch2, fpdc12, hdc1, chevron 0–6 months, sl st in first fpdc. (24)

**Rnd 9:** Ch2, 2fpdc in next st, fpdc10, 2fpdc in next st, hdc1, chevron 0–6 months, sl st in first fpdc. (26)

**Rnd 10:** Ch2, fpdc1, 2fpdc in next st, fpdc10, 2fpdc in next st, fpdc1, hdc1, chevron 0–6 months, sl st in first fpdc. (28)

**Rnd 11:** Ch2, fpdc2, 2fpdc in next st, fpdc10, 2fpdc in next st, fpdc2, hdc1, chevron 0–6 months, sl st in first fpdc. (30)

**Rnd 12:** Ch2, fpdc2, fpdc2tog, fpdc10, fpdc2tog, fpdc2, hdc1, chevron 0–6 months, sl st in first fpdc. (28)

**Rnd 13:** Ch2, fpdc1, fpdc2tog, fpdc10, fpdc2tog, fpdc1, hdc1, chevron 0–6 months, sl st in first fpdc. (26)

**Rnd 14:** Ch2, fpdc2tog, fpdc10, fpdc2tog, hdc1, chevron 0–6 months, sl st in first fpdc. (24)

**Rnd 15:** Ch2, fpdc12, hdc1 (place marker in this hdc), chevron 0–6 months, sl st in first fpdc. (24)

**Rnds 16–17:** Ch2, *fpdc1, bpdc1*, repeat from * to * to marker, {fphdc1, bphdc1}, repeat from { to } to end, sl st in first fpdc. (24)

Veiltail chevron 12-24 months motif

**SIZE: 12-24 MONTHS**

**Chevron 12-24 months:** Bpdc2, 2fpdc in next st, fpdc1, fpdc2tog, fpdc1, fpdc2tog, fpdc1, 2fpdc in next st, bpdc3.

**Rnd 1:** Start with a magic loop, ch2 (first ch2 doesn't count as first dc throughout the pattern), 6dc in the loop, sl st in first dc. (6)

**Rnd 2:** Ch2, 2fpdc in each stitch around, sl st in first fpdc. (12)

**Rnd 3:** Ch2, *fpdc1, 2fpdc in next st*, repeat * to * 2 more times, hdc1, 2fpdc in next st, repeat * to * 2 more times, sl st in first fpdc. (18)

**Rnd 4:** Ch2, *fpdc2, 2fpdc in next st*, repeat * to * 2 more times, hdc1, fpdc1, 2fpdc in next st, repeat * to * 2 more times, sl st in first fpdc. (24)

**Rnd 5:** Ch2, *fpdc3, 2fpdc in next st*, repeat * to * 2 more times, hdc1, fpdc2, 2fpdc in next st, repeat * to * 2 more times, sl st in first fpdc. (30)

**Rnds 6-13:** Ch2, fpdc15, hdc1, chevron 12-24 months, sl st in first fpdc. (30)

**Rnd 14:** Ch2, 2fpdc in next st, fpdc13, 2fpdc in next st, hdc1, chevron 12-24 months, sl st in first fpdc. (32)

**Rnd 15:** Ch2, fpdc1, 2fpdc in next st, fpdc13, 2fpdc in next st, fpdc1, hdc1, chevron 12-24 months, sl st in first fpdc. (34)

**Rnd 16:** Ch2, fpdc2, 2fpdc in next st, fpdc13, 2fpdc in next st, fpdc2, hdc1, chevron 12-24 months, sl st in first fpdc. (36)

**Rnd 17:** Ch2, fpdc3, 2fpdc in next st, fpdc13, 2fpdc in next st, fpdc3, hdc1, chevron 12-24 months, sl st in first fpdc. (38)

**Rnd 18:** Ch2, fpdc3, fpdc2tog, fpdc13, fpdc2tog, fpdc3, hdc1, chevron 12-24 months, sl st in first fpdc. (36)

**Rnd 19:** Ch2, fpdc2, fpdc2tog, fpdc13, fpdc2tog, fpdc2, hdc1, chevron 12-24 months, sl st in first fpdc. (34)

**Rnd 20:** Ch2, fpdc1, fpdc2tog, fpdc13, fpdc2tog, fpdc1, hdc1, chevron 12-24 months, sl st in first fpdc. (32)

**Rnd 21:** Ch2, fpdc2tog, fpdc13, fpdc2tog, hdc1, chevron 12-24 months, sl st in first fpdc. (30)

**Rnd 22:** Ch2, fpdc15, hdc1 (place marker in this hdc), chevron 12-24 months, sl st in first fpdc. (30)

**Rnds 23-25:** Ch2, fpdc1, *bpdc1, fpdc1*, repeat from * to * to marker, bphdc1, {fphdc1, bphdc1}, repeat from { to } to end, sl st in first fpdc. (30)

**SIZE: 3-5 YEARS**

**Chevron 3-5 years:** Bpdc2, [2fpdc in next st] 2 times, [fpdc2tog] 2 times, fpdc1, [fpdc2tog] 2 times, [2fpdc in next st] 2 times, bpdc2.

**Rnd 1:** Start with a magic loop, ch2 (first ch2 doesn't count as first dc throughout the pattern), 6dc in the loop, sl st in first dc. (6)

**Rnd 2:** Ch2, 2fpdc in each stitch around, sl st in first fpdc. (12)

**Rnd 3:** Ch2, *fpdc1, 2fpdc in next st*, repeat * to * 2 more times, hdc1, 2fpdc in next st, repeat * to * 2 more times, sl st in first fpdc. (18)

**Rnd 4:** Ch2, *fpdc2, 2fpdc in next st*, repeat * to * 2 more times, hdc1, fpdc1, 2fpdc in next st, repeat * to * 2 more times, sl st in first fpdc. (24)

**Rnd 5:** Ch2, *fpdc3, 2fpdc in next st*, repeat * to * 2 more times, hdc1, fpdc2, 2fpdc in next st, repeat * to * 2 more times, sl st in first fpdc. (30)

**Rnd 6:** Ch2, *fpdc4, 2fpdc in next st*, repeat * to * 2 more times, hdc1, fpdc3, 2fpdc in next st, repeat * to * 2 more times, sl st in first fpdc. (36)

**Rnds 7-18:** Ch2, fpdc18, hdc1, chevron 3-5 years, sl st in first fpdc. (36)

**Rnd 19:** Ch2, 2fpdc in next st, fpdc16, 2fpdc in next st, hdc1, chevron 3-5 years, sl st in first fpdc. (38)

**Rnd 20:** Ch2, fpdc1, 2fpdc in next st, fpdc16, 2fpdc in next st, fpdc1, hdc1, chevron 3-5 years, sl st in first fpdc. (40)

**Rnd 21:** Ch2, fpdc2, 2fpdc in next st, fpdc16, 2fpdc in next st, fpdc2, hdc1, chevron 3-5 years, sl st in first fpdc. (42)

**Rnd 22:** Ch2, fpdc3, 2fpdc in next st, fpdc16, 2fpdc in next st, fpdc3, hdc1, chevron 3-5 years, sl st in first fpdc. (44)

**Rnd 23:** Ch2, fpdc4, 2fpdc in next st, fpdc16, 2fpdc in next st, fpdc4, hdc1, chevron 3-5 years, sl st in first fpdc. (46)

**Rnd 24:** Ch2, fpdc4, fpdc2tog, fpdc16, fpdc2tog, fpdc4, hdc1, chevron 3-5 years, sl st in first fpdc. (44)

**Rnd 25:** Ch2, fpdc3, fpdc2tog, fpdc16, fpdc2tog, fpdc3, hdc1, chevron 3-5 years, sl st in first fpdc. (42)

**Rnd 26:** Ch2, fpdc2, fpdc2tog, fpdc16, fpdc2tog, fpdc2, hdc1, chevron 3-5 years, sl st in first fpdc. (40)

**Rnd 27:** Ch2, fpdc1, fpdc2tog, fpdc16, fpdc2tog, fpdc1, hdc1, chevron 3-5 years, sl st in first fpdc. (38)

**Rnd 28:** Ch2, fpdc2tog, fpdc16, fpdc2tog, hdc1, chevron 3-5 years, sl st in first fpdc. (36)

**Rnd 29:** Ch2, fpdc18, hdc1 (place marker in this hdc), chevron 3-5 years, sl st in first fpdc. (36)

**Rnds 30-33:** Ch2, *fpdc1, bpdc1*, repeat from * to * to marker, {fphdc1, bphdc1}, repeat from { to } to end, sl st in first fpdc. (36)

**SIZE: 6-10 YEARS**

**Chevron 6-10 years:** Bpdc2, [2fpdc in next st] 2 times, fpdc1, [fpdc2tog] 2 times, fpdc1, [fpdc2tog] 2 times, fpdc1, [2fpdc in next st] 2 times, bpdc3.

**Rnd 1:** Start with a magic loop, ch2 (first ch2 doesn't count as first dc throughout the pattern), 6dc in the loop, sl st in first dc. (6)

**Rnd 2:** Ch2, 2fpdc in each stitch around, sl st in first fpdc. (12)

**Rnd 3:** Ch2, *fpdc1, 2fpdc in next st*, repeat * to * 2 more times, hdc1, 2fpdc in next st, repeat * to * 2 more times, sl st in first fpdc. (18)

**Rnd 4:** Ch2, *fpdc2, 2fpdc in next st*, repeat * to * 2 more times, hdc1, fpdc1, 2fpdc in next st, repeat * to * 2 more times, sl st in first fpdc. (24)

**Rnd 5:** Ch2, *fpdc3, 2fpdc in next st*, repeat * to * 2 more times, hdc1, fpdc2, 2fpdc in next st, repeat * to * 2 more times, sl st in first fpdc. (30)

**Rnd 6:** Ch2, *fpdc4, 2fpdc in next st*, repeat * to * 2 more times, hdc1, fpdc3, 2fpdc in next st, repeat * to * 2 more times, sl st in first fpdc. (36)

**Rnd 7:** Ch2, *fpdc5, 2fpdc in next st*, repeat * to * 2 more times, hdc1, fpdc4, 2fpdc in next st, repeat * to * 2 more times, sl st in first fpdc. (42)

**Rnds 8-23:** Ch2, fpdc21, hdc1, chevron 6-10 years, sl st in first fpdc. (42)

**Rnd 24:** Ch2, 2fpdc in next st, fpdc19, 2fpdc in next st, hdc1, chevron 6-10 years, sl st in first fpdc. (44)

**Rnd 25:** Ch2, fpdc1, 2fpdc in next st, fpdc19, 2fpdc in next st, fpdc1, hdc1, chevron 6-10 years, sl st in first fpdc. (46)

**Rnd 26:** Ch2, fpdc2, 2fpdc in next st, fpdc19, 2fpdc in next st, fpdc2, hdc1, chevron 6-10 years, sl st in first fpdc. (48)

**Rnd 27:** Ch2, fpdc3, 2fpdc in next st, fpdc19, 2fpdc in next st, fpdc3, hdc1, chevron 6-10 years, sl st in first fpdc. (50)

**Rnd 28:** Ch2, fpdc4, 2fpdc in next st, fpdc19, 2fpdc in next st, fpdc4, hdc1, chevron 6-10 years, sl st in first fpdc. (52)

**Rnd 29:** Ch2, fpdc5, 2fpdc in next st, fpdc19, 2fpdc in next st, fpdc5, hdc1, chevron 6-10 years, sl st in first fpdc. (54)

**Rnd 30:** Ch2, fpdc5, fpdc2tog, fpdc19, fpdc2tog, fpdc5, hdc1, chevron 6-10 years, sl st in first fpdc. (52)

**Rnd 31:** Ch2, fpdc4, fpdc2tog, fpdc19, fpdc2tog, fpdc4, hdc1, chevron 6-10 years, sl st in first fpdc. (50)

**Rnd 32:** Ch2, fpdc3, fpdc2tog, fpdc19, fpdc2tog, fpdc3, hdc1, chevron 6-10 years, sl st in first fpdc. (48)

**Rnd 33:** Ch2, fpdc2, fpdc2tog, fpdc19, fpdc2tog, fpdc2, hdc1, chevron 6-10 years, sl st in first fpdc. (46)

**Rnd 34:** Ch2, fpdc1, fpdc2tog, fpdc19, fpdc2tog, fpdc1, hdc1, chevron 6-10 years, sl st in first fpdc. (44)

Veiltail chevron small motif

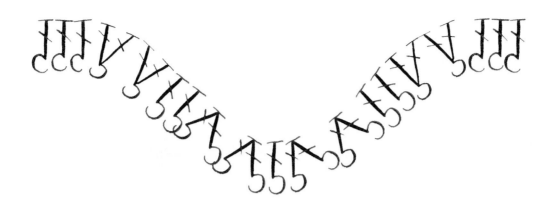

**Rnd 35:** Ch2, fpdc2tog, fpdc19, fpdc2tog, hdc1,
chevron 6-10 years, sl st in first fpdc. (42)

**Rnd 36:** Ch2, fpdc21, hdc1 (place marker in this
hdc), chevron 6-10 years, sl st in first
fpdc. (42)

**Rnds 37-41:** Ch2, fpdc1, *bpdc1, fpdc1*, repeat from
* to * to marker, bphdc1, {fphdc1, bphdc1},
repeat from { to } to end, sl st in first
fpdc. (42)


**SIZE: SMALL**

---

**Chevron small:** Bpdc3, [2fpdc in next st] 2 times,
fpdc2, [fpdc2tog] 2 times, fpdc1, [fpdc2tog] 2
times, fpdc2, [2fpdc in next st] 2 times, bpdc3.

**Rnd 1:** Start with a magic loop, ch2 (first ch2
doesn't count as first dc throughout the
pattern), 6dc in the loop, sl st in first dc.
(6)

**Rnd 2:** Ch2, 2fpdc in each stitch around, sl st in
first fpdc. (12)

**Rnd 3:** Ch2, *fpdc1, 2fpdc in next st*, repeat *
to * 2 more times, hdc1, 2fpdc in next st,
repeat * to * 2 more times, sl st in first
fpdc. (18)

**Rnd 4:** Ch2, *fpdc2, 2fpdc in next st*, repeat * to
* 2 more times, hdc1, fpdc1, 2fpdc in next
st, repeat * to * 2 more times, sl st in first
fpdc. (24)

**Rnd 5:** Ch2, *fpdc3, 2fpdc in next st*, repeat * to
* 2 more times, hdc1, fpdc2, 2fpdc in next
st, repeat * to * 2 more times, sl st in first
fpdc. (30)

**Rnd 6:** Ch2, *fpdc4, 2fpdc in next st*, repeat * to
* 2 more times, hdc1, fpdc3, 2fpdc in next
st, repeat * to * 2 more times, sl st in first
fpdc. (36)

**Rnd 7:** Ch2, *fpdc5, 2fpdc in next st*, repeat * to
* 2 more times, hdc1, fpdc4, 2fpdc in next
st, repeat * to * 2 more times, sl st in first
fpdc. (42)

**Rnd 8:** Ch2, *fpdc6, 2fpdc in next st*, repeat * to
* 2 more times, hdc1, fpdc5, 2fpdc in next
st, repeat * to * 2 more times, sl st in first
fpdc. (48)

**Rnds 9-28:** Ch2, fpdc24, hdc1, chevron small, sl st
in first fpdc. (48)

**Rnd 29:** Ch2, 2fpdc in next st, fpdc22, 2fpdc in next
st, hdc1, chevron small, sl st in first fpdc.
(50)

**Rnd 30:** Ch2, fpdc1, 2fpdc in next st, fpdc22, 2fpdc
in next st, fpdc1, hdc1, chevron small, sl
st in first fpdc. (52)

**Rnd 31:** Ch2, fpdc2, 2fpdc in next st, fpdc22, 2fpdc
in next st, fpdc2, hdc1, chevron small, sl
st in first fpdc. (54)

**Rnd 32:** Ch2, fpdc3, 2fpdc in next st, fpdc22, 2fpdc
in next st, fpdc3, hdc1, chevron small, sl
st in first fpdc. (56)

**Rnd 33:** Ch2, fpdc4, 2fpdc in next st, fpdc22, 2fpdc
in next st, fpdc4, hdc1, chevron small, sl
st in first fpdc. (58)

**Rnd 34:** Ch2, fpdc5, 2fpdc in next st, fpdc22, 2fpdc
in next st, fpdc5, hdc1, chevron small, sl
st in first fpdc. (60)

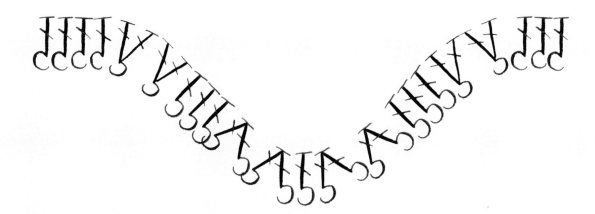

**Rnd 35:** Ch2, fpdc6, 2fpdc in next st, fpdc22, 2fpdc in next st, fpdc6, hdc1, chevron small, sl st in first fpdc. (62)

**Rnd 36:** Ch2, fpdc6, fpdc2tog, fpdc22, fpdc2tog, fpdc6, hdc1, chevron small, fpdc1, sl st in first fpdc. (60)

**Rnd 37:** Ch2, fpdc5, fpdc2tog, fpdc22, fpdc2tog, fpdc5, hdc1, chevron small, sl st in first fpdc. (58)

**Rnd 38:** Ch2, fpdc4, fpdc2tog, fpdc22, fpdc2tog, fpdc4, hdc1, chevron small, sl st in first fpdc. (56)

**Rnd 39:** Ch2, fpdc3, fpdc2tog, fpdc22, fpdc2tog, fpdc3, hdc1, chevron small, sl st in first fpdc. (54)

**Rnd 40:** Ch2, fpdc2, fpdc2tog, fpdc22, fpdc2tog, fpdc2, hdc1, chevron small, sl st in first fpdc. (52)

**Rnd 41:** Ch2, fpdc1, fpdc2tog, fpdc22, fpdc2tog, fpdc1, hdc1, chevron small, sl st in first fpdc. (50)

**Rnd 42:** Ch2, fpdc2tog, fpdc22, fpdc2tog, hdc1, chevron small, sl st in first fpdc. (48)

**Rnd 43:** Ch2, fpdc24, hdc1 (place marker in this hdc), chevron small, sl st in first fpdc. (48)

**Rnds 44-49:** Ch2, *fpdc1, bpdc1*, repeat from * to * to marker, {fphdc1, bphdc1}, repeat from { to } to end, sl st in first fpdc. (48)

---
---
---

**SIZE: MEDIUM**

---

**Chevron medium:** Bpdc3, [2fpdc in next st] 2 times, fpdc3, [fpdc2tog] 2 times, fpdc1, [fpdc2tog] 2 times, fpdc3, [2fpdc in next st] 2 times, bpdc4.

**Rnd 1:** Start with a magic loop, ch2 (first ch2 doesn't count as first dc throughout the pattern), 6dc in the loop, sl st in first dc. (6)

**Rnd 2:** Ch2, 2fpdc in each stitch around, sl st in first fpdc. (12)

**Rnd 3:** Ch2, *fpdc1, 2fpdc in next st*, repeat * to * 2 more times, hdc1, 2fpdc in next st, repeat * to * 2 more times, sl st in first fpdc. (18)

**Rnd 4:** Ch2, *fpdc2, 2fpdc in next st*, repeat * to * 2 more times, hdc1, fpdc1, 2fpdc in next st, repeat * to * 2 more times, sl st in first fpdc. (24)

**Rnd 5:** Ch2, *fpdc3, 2fpdc in next st*, repeat * to * 2 more times, hdc1, fpdc2, 2fpdc in next st, repeat * to * 2 more times, sl st in first fpdc. (30)

**Rnd 6:** Ch2, *fpdc4, 2fpdc in next st*, repeat * to * 2 more times, hdc1, fpdc3, 2fpdc in next st, repeat * to * 2 more times, sl st in first fpdc. (36)

**Rnd 7:** Ch2, *fpdc5, 2fpdc in next st*, repeat * to * 2 more times, hdc1, fpdc4, 2fpdc in next st, repeat * to * 2 more times, sl st in first fpdc. (42)

**Rnd 8:** Ch2, *fpdc6, 2fpdc in next st*, repeat * to * 2 more times, hdc1, fpdc5, 2fpdc in next st, repeat * to * 2 more times, sl st in first fpdc. (48)

**Rnd 9:** Ch2, *fpdc7, 2fpdc in next st*, repeat * to * 2 more times, hdc1, fpdc6, 2fpdc in next st, repeat * to * 2 more times, sl st in first fpdc. (54)

**Rnds 10-33:** Ch2, fpdc27, hdc1, chevron medium, sl st in first fpdc. (54)

**Rnd 34:** Ch2, 2fpdc in next st, fpdc25, 2fpdc in same st, hdc1, chevron medium, sl st in first fpdc. (56)

**Rnd 35:** Ch2, fpdc1, 2fpdc in next st, fpdc25, 2fpdc in next st, fpdc1, hdc1, chevron medium, sl st in first fpdc. (58)

**Rnd 36:** Ch2, fpdc2, 2fpdc in next st, fpdc25, 2fpdc in next st, fpdc2, hdc1, chevron medium, sl st in first fpdc. (60)

**Rnd 37:** Ch2, fpdc3, 2fpdc in next st, fpdc25, 2fpdc in next st, fpdc3, hdc1, chevron medium, sl st in first fpdc. (62)

**Rnd 38:** Ch2, fpdc4, 2fpdc in next st, fpdc25, 2fpdc in next st, fpdc4, hdc1, chevron medium, sl st in first fpdc. (64)

**Rnd 39:** Ch2, fpdc5, 2fpdc in next st, fpdc25, 2fpdc in next st, fpdc5, hdc1, chevron medium, sl st in first fpdc. (66)

**Rnd 40:** Ch2, fpdc6, 2fpdc in next st, fpdc25, 2fpdc in next st, fpdc6, hdc1, chevron medium, sl st in first fpdc. (68)

**Rnd 41:** Ch2, fpdc7, 2fpdc in next st, fpdc25, 2fpdc in next st, fpdc7, hdc1, chevron medium, sl st in first fpdc. (70)

**Rnd 42:** Ch2, fpdc7, fpdc2tog, fpdc25, fpdc2tog, fpdc7, hdc1, chevron medium, sl st in first fpdc. (68)

**Rnd 43:** Ch2, fpdc6, fpdc2tog, fpdc25, fpdc2tog, fpdc6, hdc1, chevron medium, sl st in first fpdc. (66)

**Rnd 44:** Ch2, fpdc5, fpdc2tog, fpdc25, fpdc2tog, fpdc5, hdc1, chevron medium, sl st in first fpdc. (64)

**Rnd 45:** Ch2, fpdc4, fpdc2tog, fpdc25, fpdc2tog, fpdc4, hdc1, chevron medium, sl st in first fpdc. (62)

**Rnd 46:** Ch2, fpdc3, fpdc2tog, fpdc25, fpdc2tog, fpdc3, hdc1,chevron medium, sl st in first fpdc. (60)

**Rnd 47:** Ch2, fpdc2, fpdc2tog, fpdc25, fpdc2tog, fpdc2, hdc1, chevron medium, sl st in first fpdc. (58)

**Rnd 48:** Ch2, fpdc1, fpdc2tog, fpdc25, fpdc2tog, fpdc1, hdc1, chevron medium, sl st in first fpdc. (56)

**Rnd 49:** Ch2, fpdc2tog, fpdc25, fpdc2tog, hdc1, chevron medium, sl st in first fpdc. (54)

**Rnd 50:** Ch2, fpdc27, hdc1 (place marker in this hdc), chevron medium, sl st in first fpdc. (54)

**Rnds 51-57:** Ch2, fpdc1, *bpdc1, fpdc1*, repeat from * to * to marker, bphdc1, {fphdc1, bphdc1}, repeat from { to } to end, sl st in first fpdc. (54)

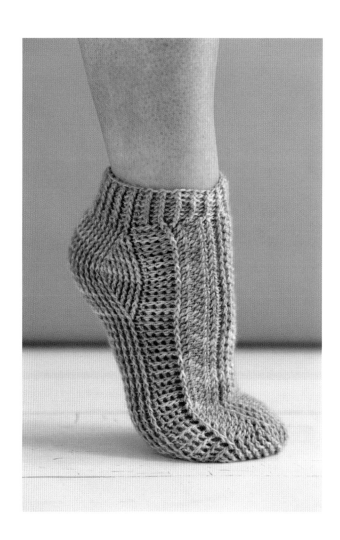

# cable car

CABLED SOCKS ARE A HANDMADE FAVORITE, AND THESE SOCKS ARE SO MUCH FUN TO CROCHET! THE PATTERN TAKES A BIT OF PRACTICE TO MASTER, BUT ONCE YOUR FINGERS LEARN THE MOTIONS, YOU'LL ENJOY THE PROCESS AND THE FINISHED MASTERPIECE.

For help in choosing the right size, see page 15.
For help in choosing the right hook size and checking gauge, see page 16.

## MATERIALS

**Yarn**

**Cream socks:** Lana Grossa Meilenweit Tweed, #1 super fine weight (80% virgin wool, 20% polyamide; 459 yd./420 m per 3.5 oz./100 g); color #106

**Gray socks:** Regia 4-Ply Sock Tweed (70% wool, 5% viscose, 25% polyamide; 425 yd./400 m per 3.5 oz./100 g); color #0090

**Hook**
US size G-6 (4 mm)

**Gauge**
5 fpdc wide and 4 rnds high = 0.7 in./2 cm

**Estimated total yarn required**
12–24 months: 230 yd./210 m; 3–5 years: 460 yd./420 m; 6–10 years: 460 yd./420 m; Small: 689 yd./630 m; Medium: 689 yd./630 m

## ABBREVIATIONS

| | | |
|---|---|---|
| ⌒ | **ch** | chain |
| ⊤ | **dc** | double crochet |
| ⌶ | **fpdc** | front post double crochet |
| ⌶ | **fptrc** | front post triple crochet |
| ⌡ | **bpdc** | back post double crochet |
| ● | **sl st** | slip stitch |
| ⊤ | **hdc** | half double crochet |
| Å | **fpdc2tog** | front post double crochet 2 together (1 stitch decreased) |
| V | **2 fpdc in the next stitch** | 2 fpdc in the same stitch (1 stitch increased) |

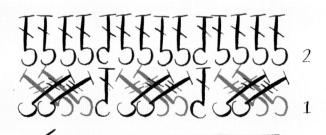

**SIZE: 12-24 MONTHS**

**Cable 12-24 motif 1:** *Skip 2 stitches, fptrc2, fptrc1 in each of the 2 stitches you just skipped behind your previous 2 fptrc*, bpdc1, repeat from * to * 1 time, bpdc1, repeat from * to * 1 time.

**Cable 12-24 motif 2:** Fpdc4, bpdc1, fpdc4, bpdc1, fpdc4.

**Rnd 1:**  Start with a magic loop, ch2 (first ch2 doesn't count as first dc throughout the pattern), 6dc in the loop, sl st in first dc. (6)

**Rnd 2:**  Ch2, 2fpdc in each stitch around, sl st in first fpdc. (12)

**Rnd 3:**  Ch2, *fpdc1, 2fpdc in next st*, repeat * to * 2 more times, hdc1, 2fpdc in next st, repeat * to * 2 more times, sl st in first fpdc. (18)

**Rnd 4:**  Ch2, *fpdc2, 2fpdc in next st*, repeat * to * 2 more times, hdc1, fpdc1, 2fpdc in same st, repeat * to * 2 more times, sl st in first fpdc. (24)

**Rnd 5:**  Ch2, *fpdc3, 2fpdc in next st*, repeat * to * 2 more times, hdc1, fpdc2, 2fpdc in next st, repeat * to * 2 more times, sl st in first fpdc. (30)

**Rnd 6:**  Ch2, fpdc15, hdc1, cable 12-24 motif 1, sl st in first fpdc. (30)

**Rnd 7:**  Ch2, fpdc15, hdc1, cable 12-24 motif 2, sl st in first fpdc. (30)

**Rnd 8:**  Ch2, fpdc15, hdc1, cable 12-24 motif 2, sl st in first fpdc. (30)

**Rnds 9-17:** Repeat Rnds 6-8.

**Rnd 18:**  Ch2, 2fpdc in next st, fpdc13, 2fpdc in next st, hdc1, cable 12-24 motif 1, sl st in first fpdc. (32)

**Rnd 19:**  Ch2, fpdc1, 2fpdc in next st, fpdc13, 2fpdc in next st, fpdc1, hdc1, cable 12-24 motif 2, sl st in first fpdc. (34)

**Rnd 20:**  Ch2, fpdc2, 2fpdc in next st, fpdc13, 2fpdc in next st, fpdc2, hdc1, cable 12-24 motif 2, sl st in first fpdc. (36)

**Rnd 21:**  Ch2, fpdc3, 2fpdc in next st, fpdc13, 2fpdc in next st, fpdc3, hdc1, cable 12-24 motif 1, sl st in first fpdc. (38)

**Rnd 22:**  Ch2, fpdc3, fpdc2tog, fpdc13, fpdc2tog, fpdc3, hdc1, cable 12-24 motif 2, sl st in first fpdc. (36)

**Rnd 23:**  Ch2, fpdc2, fpdc2tog, fpdc13, fpdc2tog, fpdc2, hdc1, cable 12-24 motif 2, sl st in first fpdc. (34)

**Rnd 24:**  Ch2, fpdc1, fpdc2tog, fpdc13, fpdc2tog, fpdc1, hdc1, cable 12-24 motif 1, sl st in first fpdc. (32)

**Rnd 25:**  Ch2, fpdc2tog, fpdc13, fpdc2tog, hdc1, cable 12-24 motif 2, sl st in first fpdc. (30)

**Rnd 26:**  Ch2, fpdc15, hdc1, cable 12-24 motif 2, sl st in first fpdc. (30)

**Rnds 27-31:** Repeat Rnds 6-8 (you'll end with Rnd 7).

**Rnds 32-34:** Ch2, *fpdc1, bpdc1*, repeat * to * around, sl st in first fpdc. (30)

Fasten off and weave in ends.

**SIZE: 3–5 YEARS**

**Cable 3–5 motif 1:** *Bpdc1, skip 2 stitches, fptrc2, fptrc1 in each of the 2 stitches you just skipped behind your previous 2 fptrc*, repeat from * to * 2 times, bpdc2.

**Cable 3–5 motif 2:** Bpdc1, fpdc4, bpdc1, fpdc4, bpdc1, fpdc4, bpdc2.

**Rnd 1:** Start with a magic loop, ch2 (first ch2 doesn't count as first dc throughout the pattern), 6dc in the loop, sl st in first dc. (6)

**Rnd 2:** Ch2, 2fpdc in each stitch around, sl st in first fpdc. (12)

**Rnd 3:** Ch2, *fpdc1, 2fpdc in next st*, repeat * to * 2 more times, hdc1, 2fpdc in next st, repeat * to * 2 more times, sl st in first fpdc. (18)

**Rnd 4:** Ch2, *fpdc2, 2fpdc in next st*, repeat * to * 2 more times, hdc1, fpdc1, 2fpdc in next st, repeat * to * 2 more times, sl st in first fpdc. (24)

**Rnd 5:** Ch2, *fpdc3, 2fpdc in next st*, repeat * to * 2 more times, hdc1, fpdc2, 2fpdc in next st, repeat * to * 2 more times, sl st in first fpdc. (30)

**Rnd 6:** Ch2, *fpdc4, 2fpdc in next st*, repeat * to * 2 more times, hdc1, fpdc3, 2fpdc in next st, repeat * to * 2 more times, sl st in first fpdc. (36)

**Rnd 7:** Ch2, fpdc18, hdc1, cable 3–5 motif 1, sl st in first fpdc. (36)

**Rnd 8:** Ch2, fpdc18, hdc1, cable 3–5 motif 2, sl st in first fpdc. (36)

**Rnd 9:** Ch2, fpdc18, hdc1, cable 3–5 motif 2, sl st in first fpdc. (36)

**Rnds 10–21:** Repeat Rnds 7–9.

**Rnd 22:** Ch2, fpdc18, hdc1, cable 3–5 motif 1, sl st in first fpdc. (36)

**Rnd 23:** Ch2, 2fpdc in next st, fpdc16, 2fpdc in next st, hdc1, cable 3–5 motif 2, sl st in first fpdc. (38)

**Rnd 24:** Ch2, fpdc1, 2fpdc in next st, fpdc16, 2fpdc in next st, fpdc1, hdc1, cable 3–5 motif 2, sl st in first fpdc. (40)

**Rnd 25:** Ch2, fpdc2, 2fpdc in next st, fpdc16, 2fpdc in next st, fpdc2, hdc1, cable 3–5 motif 1, sl st in first fpdc. (42)

**Rnd 26:** Ch2, fpdc3, 2fpdc in next st, fpdc16, 2fpdc in next st, fpdc3, hdc1, cable 3–5 motif 2, sl st in first fpdc. (44)

**Rnd 27:** Ch2, fpdc4, 2fpdc in next st, fpdc16, 2fpdc in next st, fpdc4, hdc1, cable 3–5 motif 2, sl st in first fpdc. (46)

**Rnd 28:** Ch2, fpdc4, fpdc2tog, fpdc16, fpdc2tog, fpdc4, hdc1, cable 3–5 motif 1, sl st in first fpdc. (44)

**Rnd 29:** Ch2, fpdc3, fpdc2tog, fpdc16, fpdc2tog, fpdc3, hdc1, cable 3–5 motif 2, sl st in first fpdc. (42)

**Rnd 30:** Ch2, fpdc2, fpdc2tog, fpdc16, fpdc2tog, fpdc2, hdc1, cable 3–5 motif 2, sl st in first fpdc. (40)

**Rnd 31:** Ch2, fpdc1, fpdc2tog, fpdc16, fpdc2tog, fpdc1, hdc1, cable 3–5 motif 1, sl st in first fpdc. (38)

**Rnd 32:** Ch2, fpdc2tog, fpdc16, fpdc2tog, hdc1, cable 3–5 motif 2, sl st in first fpdc. (36)

Fasten off and weave in ends.

2

1

## SIZE: 6-10 YEARS

**Cable 6-10 motif 1:** *Bpdc2, skip 2 stitches, fptrc2, fptrc1 in each of the 2 stitches you just skipped behind your previous 2 fptrc*, repeat from * to * 2 times, bpdc2.

**Cable 6-10 motif 2:** Bpdc2, fpdc4, bpdc2, fpdc4, bpdc2, fpdc4, bpdc2.

**Rnd 1:** Start with a magic loop, ch2 (first ch2 doesn't count as first dc throughout the pattern), 6dc in the loop, sl st in first dc. (6)

**Rnd 2:** Ch2, 2fpdc in each stitch around, sl st in first fpdc. (12)

**Rnd 3:** Ch2, *fpdc1, 2fpdc in next st*, repeat * to * 2 more times, hdc1, 2fpdc in next st, repeat * to * 2 more times, sl st in first fpdc. (18)

**Rnd 4:** Ch2, *fpdc2, 2fpdc in next st*, repeat * to * 2 more times, hdc1, fpdc1, 2fpdc in next st, repeat * to * 2 more times, sl st in first fpdc. (24)

**Rnd 5:** Ch2, *fpdc3, 2fpdc in next st*, repeat * to * 2 more times, hdc1, fpdc2, 2fpdc in next st, repeat * to * 2 more times, sl st in first fpdc. (30)

**Rnd 6:** Ch2, *fpdc4, 2fpdc in next st*, repeat * to * 2 more times, hdc1, fpdc3, 2fpdc in next st, repeat * to * 2 more times, sl st in first fpdc. (36)

**Rnd 7:** Ch2, *fpdc5, 2fpdc in next st*, repeat * to * 2 more times, hdc1, fpdc4, 2fpdc in next st, repeat * to * 2 more times, sl st in first fpdc. (42)

**Rnd 8:** Ch2, fpdc21, hdc1, cable 6-10 motif 1, sl st in first fpdc. (42)

**Rnd 9:** Ch2, fpdc21, hdc1, cable 6-10 motif 2, sl st in first fpdc. (42)

**Rnd 10:** Ch2, fpdc21, hdc1, cable 6-10 motif 2, sl st in first fpdc. (42)

**Rnds 11-27:** Repeat Rnds 8-10 (you'll end with Rnd 9).

**Rnd 28:** Ch2, fpdc21, hdc1, cable 6-10 motif 2, sl st in first fpdc. (42)

**Rnd 29:** Ch2, 2fpdc in next st, fpdc19, 2fpdc in next st, hdc1, cable 6-10 motif 1, sl st in first fpdc. (44)

**Rnd 30:** Ch2, fpdc1, 2fpdc in next st, fpdc19, 2fpdc in next st, fpdc1, hdc1, cable 6-10 motif 2, sl st in first fpdc. (46)

**Rnd 31:** Ch2, fpdc2, 2fpdc in next st, fpdc19, 2fpdc in next st, fpdc2, hdc1, cable 6-10 motif 2, sl st in first fpdc. (48)

**Rnd 32:** Ch2, fpdc3, 2fpdc in next st, fpdc19, 2fpdc in next st, fpdc3, hdc1, cable 6-10 motif 1, sl st in first fpdc. (50)

**Rnd 33:** Ch2, fpdc4, 2fpdc in next st, fpdc19, 2fpdc in next st, fpdc4, hdc1, cable 6-10 motif 2, sl st in first fpdc. (52)

**Rnd 34:** Ch2, fpdc5, 2fpdc in next st, fpdc19, 2fpdc in next st, fpdc5, hdc1, cable 6-10 motif 2, sl st in first fpdc. (54)

**Rnd 35:** Ch2, fpdc5, fpdc2tog, fpdc19, fpdc2tog, fpdc5, hdc1, cable 6-10 motif 1, sl st in first fpdc. (52)

**Rnd 36:** Ch2, fpdc4, fpdc2tog, fpdc19, fpdc2tog, fpdc4, hdc1, cable 6-10 motif 2, sl st in first fpdc. (50)

**Rnd 37:** Ch2, fpdc3, fpdc2tog, fpdc19, fpdc2tog, fpdc3, hdc1, cable 6-10 motif 2, sl st in first fpdc. (48)

**Rnd 38:** Ch2, fpdc2, fpdc2tog, fpdc19, fpdc2tog, fpdc2, hdc1, cable 6-10 motif 1, sl st in first fpdc. (46)

**Rnd 39:** Ch2, fpdc1, fpdc2tog, fpdc19, fpdc2tog, fpdc1, hdc1, cable 6-10 motif 2, sl st in first fpdc. (44)

**Rnd 40:** Ch2, fpdc2tog, fpdc19, fpdc2tog, hdc1, cable 6-10 motif 2, sl st in first fpdc. (42)

**Rnd 41:** Ch2, fpdc21, hdc1, cable 6-10 motif 1, sl st in first fpdc. (42)

**Rnd 42:** Ch2, fpdc21, hdc1, cable 6-10 motif 2, sl st in first fpdc. (42)

**Rnd 43:** Ch2, fpdc21, hdc1, cable 6-10 motif 2, sl st in first fpdc. (42)

**Rnds 44-48:** Repeat Rnds 8-10 (you'll end with Rnd 9).

**Rnds 49-54:** Ch2, *fpdc1, bpdc1*, repeat * to * around, sl st in first fpdc. (42)

Fasten off and weave in ends.

**SIZE: SMALL**

**Cable small motif 1:** *Bpdc1, skip 3 stitches, fptrc3, fptrc1 in each of the 3 skipped stitches you just skipped behind your previous 3 fptrc*, repeat from * to * 2 times, bpdc2.

**Cable small motif 2:** Bpdc1, fpdc6, bpdc1, fpdc6, bpdc1, fpdc6, bpdc2.

**Rnd 1:** Start with a magic loop, ch2 (first ch2 doesn't count as first dc throughout the pattern), 6dc in the loop, sl st in first dc. (6)

**Rnd 2:** Ch2, 2fpdc in each stitch around, sl st in first fpdc. (12)

**Rnd 3:** Ch2, *fpdc1, 2fpdc in next st*, repeat * to * 2 more times, hdc1, 2fpdc in next st, repeat * to * 2 more times, sl st in first fpdc. (18)

**Rnd 4:** Ch2, *fpdc2, 2fpdc in next st*, repeat * to * 2 more times, hdc1, fpdc1, 2fpdc in next st, repeat * to * 2 more times, sl st in first fpdc. (24)

**Rnd 5:** Ch2, *fpdc3, 2fpdc in next st*, repeat * to * 2 more times, hdc1, fpdc2, 2fpdc in next st, repeat * to * 2 more times, sl st in first fpdc. (30)

**Rnd 6:** Ch2, *fpdc4, 2fpdc in next st*, repeat * to * 2 more times, hdc1, fpdc3, 2fpdc in next st, repeat * to * 2 more times, sl st in first fpdc. (36)

**Rnd 7:** Ch2, *fpdc5, 2fpdc in next st*, repeat * to * 2 more times, hdc1, fpdc4, 2fpdc in next st, repeat * to * 2 more times, sl st in first fpdc. (42)

**Rnd 8:** Ch2, *fpdc6, 2fpdc in next st*, repeat * to * 2 more times, hdc1, fpdc5, 2fpdc in next st, repeat * to * 2 more times, sl st in first fpdc. (48)

**Rnd 9:** Ch2, fpdc24, hdc1, cable small motif 1, sl st in first fpdc. (48)

**Rnd 10:** Ch2, fpdc24, hdc1, cable small motif 2, sl st in first fpdc. (48)

**Rnd 11:** Ch2, fpdc24, hdc1, cable small motif 2, sl st in first fpdc. (48)

**Rnd 12:** Ch2, fpdc24, hdc1, cable small motif 2, sl st in first fpdc. (48)

**Rnds 13–32:** Repeat Rnds 9–12.

**Rnd 33:** Ch2, 2fpdc in next st, fpdc22, 2fpdc in next st, hdc1, cable small motif 1, sl st in first fpdc. (50)

**Rnd 34:** Ch2, fpdc1, 2fpdc in next st, fpdc22, 2fpdc in next st, fpdc1, hdc1, cable small motif 2, sl st in first fpdc. (52)

**Rnd 35:** Ch2, fpdc2, 2fpdc in next st, fpdc22, 2fpdc in next st, fpdc2, hdc1, cable small motif 2, sl st in first fpdc. (54)

**Rnd 36:** Ch2, fpdc3, 2fpdc in next st, fpdc22, 2fpdc in next st, fpdc3, hdc1, cable small motif 2, sl st in first fpdc. (56)

**Rnd 37:** Ch2, fpdc4, 2fpdc in next st, fpdc22, 2fpdc in next st, fpdc4, hdc1, cable small motif 1, sl st in first fpdc. (58)

**Rnd 38:** Ch2, fpdc5, 2fpdc in next st, fpdc22, 2fpdc in next st, fpdc5, hdc1, cable small motif 2, sl st in first fpdc. (60)

**Rnd 39:** Ch2, fpdc6, 2fpdc in next st, fpdc22, 2fpdc in next st, fpdc6, hdc1, cable small motif 2, sl st in first fpdc. (62)

**Rnd 40:** Ch2, fpdc6, fpdc2tog, fpdc22, fpdc2tog, fpdc6, hdc1, cable small motif 2, sl st in first fpdc. (60)

**Rnd 41:** Ch2, fpdc5, fpdc2tog, fpdc22, fpdc2tog, fpdc5, hdc1, cable small motif 1, sl st in first fpdc. (58)

Cable car medium motifs

2

1

**Rnd 42:** Ch2, fpdc4, fpdc2tog, fpdc22, fpdc2tog,
fpdc4, hdc1, cable small motif 2, sl st in
first fpdc. (56)

**Rnd 43:** Ch2, fpdc3, fpdc2tog, fpdc22, fpdc2tog,
fpdc3, hdc1, cable small motif 2, sl st in
first fpdc. (54)

**Rnd 44:** Ch2, fpdc2, fpdc2tog, fpdc22, fpdc2tog,
fpdc2, hdc1, cable small motif 2, sl st in
first fpdc. (52)

**Rnd 45:** Ch2, fpdc1, fpdc2tog, fpdc22, fpdc2tog,
fpdc1, hdc1, cable small motif 1, sl st in
first fpdc. (50)

**Rnd 46:** Ch2, fpdc2tog, fpdc22, fpdc2tog, hdc1,
cable small motif 2, sl st in first fpdc.
(48)

**Rnd 47:** Ch2, fpdc24, hdc1, cable small motif 2, sl
st in first fpdc. (48)

**Rnd 48:** Ch2, fpdc24, hdc1, cable small motif 2, sl
st in first fpdc. (48)

**Rnds 49-56:** Repeat Rnds 9-12.

**Rnds 57-64:** Ch2, *fpdc1, bpdc1*, repeat * to *
around, sl st in first fpdc. (48)

Fasten off and weave in ends.


**SIZE: MEDIUM**

_____


**Cable medium motif 1:** *Bpdc2, skip 3 stitches,
fptrc3, fptrc1 in each of the 3 stitches you just
skipped behind your previous 3 fptrc*, repeat from
* to * two times, bpdc2.

**Cable medium motif 2:** Bpdc2, fpdc6, bpdc2, fpdc6,
bpdc2, fpdc6, bpdc2.

**Rnd 1:** Start with a magic loop, ch2 (first ch2
doesn't count as first dc throughout the
pattern), 6dc in the loop, sl st in first
dc. (6)

**Rnd 2:** Ch2, 2fpdc in each stitch around, sl st in
first fpdc. (12)

**Rnd 3:** Ch2, *fpdc1, 2fpdc in next st*, repeat *
to * 2 more times, hdc1, 2fpdc in next st,
repeat * to * 2 more times, sl st in first
fpdc. (18)

**Rnd 4:** Ch2, *fpdc2, 2fpdc in next st*, repeat * to
* 2 more times, hdc1, fpdc1, 2fpdc in next
st, repeat * to * 2 more times, sl st in first
fpdc. (24)

**Rnd 5:** Ch2, *fpdc3, 2fpdc in next st*, repeat * to
* 2 more times, hdc1, fpdc2, 2fpdc in next
st, repeat * to * 2 more times, sl st in first
fpdc. (30)

**Rnd 6:** Ch2, *fpdc4, 2fpdc in next st*, repeat * to
* 2 more times, hdc1, fpdc3, 2fpdc in next
st, repeat * to * 2 more times, sl st in first
fpdc. (36)

**Rnd 7:** Ch2, *fpdc5, 2fpdc in next st*, repeat * to
* 2 more times, hdc1, fpdc4, 2fpdc in next
st, repeat * to * 2 more times, sl st in first
fpdc. (42)

**Rnd 8:** Ch2, *fpdc6, 2fpdc in next st*, repeat * to
* 2 more times, hdc1, fpdc5, 2fpdc in next
st, repeat * to * 2 more times, sl st in first
fpdc. (48)

**Rnd 9:** Ch2, *fpdc7, 2fpdc in next st*, repeat * to
* 2 more times, hdc1, fpdc6, 2fpdc in next
st, repeat * to * 2 more times, sl st in first
fpdc. (54)

**Rnd 10:** Ch2, fpdc27, hdc1, cable medium motif 1, sl st in first fpdc. (54)

**Rnd 11:** Ch2, fpdc27, hdc1, cable medium motif 2, sl st in first fpdc. (54)

**Rnd 12:** Ch2, fpdc27, hdc1, cable medium motif 2, sl st in first fpdc. (54)

**Rnd 13:** Ch2, fpdc27, hdc1, cable medium motif 2, sl st in first fpdc. (54)

**Rnds 14–37:** Repeat Rnds 10–13.

**Rnd 38:** Ch2, 2fpdc in next st, fpdc25, 2fpdc in next st, hdc1, cable medium motif 1, sl st in first fpdc. (56)

**Rnd 39:** Ch2, fpdc1, 2fpdc in next st, fpdc25, 2fpdc in next st, fpdc1, hdc1, cable medium motif 2, sl st in first fpdc. (58)

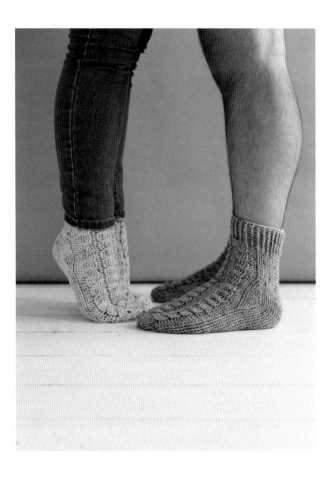

**Rnd 40:** Ch2, fpdc2, 2fpdc in next st, fpdc25, 2fpdc in next st, fpdc2, hdc1, cable medium motif 2, sl st in first fpdc. (60)

**Rnd 41:** Ch2, fpdc3, 2fpdc in next st, fpdc25, 2fpdc in next st, fpdc3, hdc1, cable medium motif 2, sl st in first fpdc. (62)

**Rnd 42:** Ch2, fpdc4, 2fpdc in next st, fpdc25, 2fpdc in next st, fpdc4, hdc1, cable medium motif 1, sl st in first fpdc. (64)

**Rnd 43:** Ch2, fpdc5, 2fpdc in next st, fpdc25, 2fpdc in next st, fpdc5, hdc1, cable medium motif 2, sl st in first fpdc. (66)

**Rnd 44:** Ch2, fpdc6, 2fpdc in next st, fpdc25, 2fpdc in next st, fpdc6, hdc1, cable medium motif 2, sl st in first fpdc. (68)

**Rnd 45:** Ch2, fpdc7, 2fpdc in next st, fpdc25, 2fpdc in next st, fpdc7, hdc1, cable medium motif 2, sl st in first fpdc. (70)

**Rnd 46:** Ch2, fpdc7, fpdc2tog, fpdc25, fpdc2tog, fpdc7, hdc1, cable medium motif 1, sl st in first fpdc. (68)

**Rnd 47:** Ch2, fpdc6, fpdc2tog, fpdc25, fpdc2tog, fpdc6, hdc1, cable medium motif 2, sl st in first fpdc. (66)

**Rnd 48:** Ch2, fpdc5, fpdc2tog, fpdc25, fpdc2tog, fpdc5, hdc1, cable medium motif 2, sl st in first fpdc. (64)

**Rnd 49:** Ch2, fpdc4, fpdc2tog, fpdc25, fpdc2tog, fpdc4, hdc1, cable medium motif 2, sl st in first fpdc. (62)

**Rnd 50:** Ch2, fpdc3, fpdc2tog, fpdc25, fpdc2tog, fpdc3, hdc1, cable medium motif 1, sl st in first fpdc. (60)

**Rnd 51:** Ch2, fpdc2, fpdc2tog, fpdc25, fpdc2tog, fpdc2, hdc1, cable medium motif 2, sl st in first fpdc. (58)

**Rnd 52:** Ch2, fpdc1, fpdc2tog, fpdc25, fpdc2tog, fpdc1, hdc1, cable medium motif 2, sl st in first fpdc. (56)

**Rnd 53:** Ch2, fpdc2tog, fpdc25, fpdc2tog, hdc1, cable medium motif 2, sl st in first fpdc. (54)

**Rnds 54–65:** Repeat Rnds 10–13.

**Rnds 66–74:** Ch2, *fpdc1, bpdc1*, repeat * to * around, sl st in first fpdc. (54)

Fasten off and weave in ends.

# crane

THESE ARE THE PERFECT YOGA SOCKS, BUT OF COURSE ALSO ARE
COMFY FOR LOUNGING ON THE SOFA, IN BED, OR WHEREVER YOU
WANT. THEY HAVE A HIGHER LEG AND MAKE NICE SLIPPER-SOCKS.

For help in choosing the right size, see page 15.
For help in choosing the right hook size and checking gauge, see page 16.

## MATERIALS

**Yarn**

**Gray socks:**  Scheepjes Invicta Extra, #1 super fine weight
(75% superwash wool, 25% nylon; 230 yd./210 m
per 1.75 oz./50 g); color #1443

**Beige socks:**  Scheepjes Invicta Extra, #1 super fine weight
(75% superwash wool, 25% nylon; 230 yd./210 m
per 1.75 oz./50 g); color #1402

**Hook**
US size G-6 (4 mm)

**Gauge**
5 fpdc wide and 4 rnds high = 0.7 in./2 cm

**Estimated total yarn required**
0–6 months: 230 yd./210 m; 12–24 months: 230 yd./210 m; 3–5
years: 460 yd./420 m; 6–10 years: 460 yd./420 m; Small: 689
yd./630 m; Medium: 919 yd./840 m; Large: 919 yd./840 m

## ABBREVIATIONS

| | | |
|---|---|---|
| ⌒ | **ch** | chain |
| ┬ | **dc** | double crochet |
| ↿ | **fpdc** | front post double crochet |
| ⇂ | **bpdc** | back post double crochet |
| ● | **sl st** | slip stitch |
| A | **fpdc2tog** | front post double crochet 2 together (1 stitch decreased) |
| V | **2 fpdc in the next stitch** | 2 fpdc in the same stitch (1 stitch increased) |

## SIZE: 0-6 MONTHS

**Rnd 1:** Start with a magic loop, ch2 (first ch2 doesn't count as first dc throughout the pattern), 6dc in the loop, sl st in first dc. (6)

**Rnd 2:** Ch2, 2fpdc in each stitch around, sl st in first fpdc. (12)

**Rnd 3:** Ch2, *fpdc1, 2fpdc in next st*, repeat * to * 2 more times, hdc1, 2fpdc in next st, repeat * to * 2 more times, sl st in first fpdc. (18)

**Rnd 4:** Ch2, *fpdc2, 2fpdc in next st*, repeat * to * 2 more times, hdc1, fpdc1, 2fpdc in next st, repeat * to * 2 more times, sl st in first fpdc. (24)

**Rnds 5-12:** Ch2, fpdc12, hdc1, fpdc11, sl st in first fpdc. (24)

**Rnd 13:** Ch2, 2fpdc in next st, fpdc10, 2fpdc in next st, hdc1, fpdc11, sl st in first fpdc. (26)

**Rnd 14:** Ch2, fpdc1, 2fpdc in next st, fpdc10, 2fpdc in next st, fpdc1, hdc1, fpdc11, sl st in first fpdc. (28)

**Rnd 15:** Ch2, fpdc2, 2fpdc in next st, fpdc10, 2fpdc in next st, fpdc2, hdc1, fpdc11, sl st in first fpdc. (30)

**Rnd 16:** Ch2, fpdc2, fpdc2tog, fpdc10, fpdc2tog, fpdc2, hdc1, fpdc11, sl st in first fpdc. (28)

**Rnd 17:** Ch2, fpdc1, fpdc2tog, fpdc10, fpdc2tog, fpdc1, hdc1, fpdc11, sl st in first fpdc. (26)

**Rnd 18:** Ch2, fpdc2tog, fpdc10, fpdc2tog, hdc1, fpdc11, sl st in first fpdc. (24)

**Rnds 19-30:** Ch2, *fpdc3, bpdc3*, repeat * to * around, sl st in first fpdc. (24)

Fasten off and weave in ends.

## SIZE: 12-24 MONTHS

**Rnd 1:** Start with a magic loop, ch2 (first ch2 doesn't count as first dc throughout the pattern), 6dc in the loop, sl st in first dc. (6)

**Rnd 2:** Ch2, 2fpdc in each stitch around, sl st in first fpdc. (12)

**Rnd 3:** Ch2, *fpdc1, 2fpdc in next st*, repeat * to * 2 more times, hdc1, 2fpdc in next st, repeat * to * 2 more times, sl st in first fpdc. (18)

**Rnd 4:** Ch2, *fpdc2, 2fpdc in next st*, repeat * to * 2 more times, hdc1, fpdc1, 2fpdc in next st, repeat * to * 2 more times, sl st in first fpdc. (24)

**Rnd 5:** Ch2, *fpdc3, 2fpdc in next st*, repeat * to * 2 more times, hdc1, fpdc2, 2fpdc in next st, repeat * to * 2 more times, sl st in first fpdc. (30)

**Rnds 6-17:** Ch2, fpdc15, hdc1, fpdc14, sl st in first fpdc. (30)

**Rnd 18:** Ch2, 2fpdc in next st, fpdc13, 2fpdc in next st, hdc1, fpdc14, sl st in first fpdc. (32)

**Rnd 19:** Ch2, fpdc1, 2fpdc in next st, fpdc13, 2fpdc in next st, fpdc1, hdc1, fpdc14, sl st in first fpdc. (34)

**Rnd 20:** Ch2, fpdc2, 2fpdc in next st, fpdc13, 2fpdc in next st, fpdc2, hdc1, fpdc14, sl st in first fpdc. (36)

**Rnd 21:** Ch2, fpdc3, 2fpdc in next st, fpdc13, 2fpdc in next st, fpdc3, hdc1, fpdc14, sl st in first fpdc. (38)

**Rnd 22:** Ch2, fpdc3, fpdc2tog, fpdc13, fpdc2tog, fpdc3, hdc1, fpdc14, sl st in first fpdc. (36)

**Rnd 23:** Ch2, fpdc2, fpdc2tog, fpdc13, fpdc2tog, fpdc2, hdc1, fpdc14, sl st in first fpdc. (34)

**Rnd 24:** Ch2, fpdc1, fpdc2tog, fpdc13, fpdc2tog, fpdc1, hdc1, fpdc14, sl st in first fpdc. (32)

**Rnd 25:** Ch2, fpdc2tog, fpdc13, fpdc2tog, hdc1, fpdc14, sl st in first fpdc. (30)

**Rnds 26-42:** Ch2, *fpdc3, bpdc3*, repeat * to * around, sl st in first fpdc. (30)

Fasten off and weave in ends.

## SIZE: 12-24 MONTHS

**Rnd 1:** Start with a magic loop, ch2 (first ch2 doesn't count as first dc throughout the pattern), 6dc in the loop, sl st in first dc. (6)

**Rnd 2:** Ch2, 2fpdc in each stitch around, sl st in first fpdc. (12)

## SIZE: 3-5 YEARS

**Rnd 1:** Start with a magic loop, ch2 (first ch2 doesn't count as first dc throughout the pattern), 6dc in the loop, sl st in first dc. (6)

**Rnd 2:** Ch2, 2fpdc in each stitch around, sl st in first fpdc. (12)

**Rnd 3:** Ch2, *fpdc1, 2fpdc in next st*, repeat * to * 2 more times, hdc1, 2fpdc in next st, repeat * to * 2 more times, sl st in first fpdc. (18)

**Rnd 4:** Ch2, *fpdc2, 2fpdc in*, repeat * to * 2 more times, hdc1, fpdc1, 2fpdc in next st, repeat * to * 2 more times, sl st in first fpdc. (24)

**Rnd 5:** Ch2, *fpdc3, 2fpdc in next st*, repeat * to * 2 more times, hdc1, fpdc2, 2fpdc in next st, repeat * to * 2 more times, sl st in first fpdc. (30)

**Rnd 6:** Ch2, *fpdc4, 2fpdc in next st*, repeat * to * 2 more times, hdc1, fpdc3, 2fpdc in next st, repeat * to * 2 more times, sl st in first fpdc. (36)

**Rnds 7-22:** Ch2, fpdc18, hdc1, fpdc17, sl st in first fpdc. (36)

**Rnd 23:** Ch2, 2fpdc in next st, fpdc16, 2fpdc in next st, hdc1, fpdc17, sl st in first fpdc. (38)

**Rnd 24:** Ch2, fpdc1, 2fpdc in next st, fpdc16, 2fpdc in next st, fpdc1, hdc1, fpdc17, sl st in first fpdc. (40)

**Rnd 25:** Ch2, fpdc2, 2fpdc in next st, fpdc16, 2fpdc in next st, fpdc2, hdc1, fpdc17, sl st in first fpdc. (42)

**Rnd 26:** Ch2, fpdc3, 2fpdc in next st, fpdc16, 2fpdc in next st, fpdc3, hdc1, fpdc17, sl st in first fpdc. (44)

**Rnd 27:** Ch2, fpdc4, 2fpdc in next st, fpdc16, 2fpdc in next st, fpdc4, hdc1, fpdc17, sl st in first fpdc. (46)

**Rnd 28:** Ch2, fpdc4, fpdc2tog, fpdc16, fpdc2tog, fpdc4, hdc1, fpdc17, sl st in first fpdc. (44)

**Rnd 29:** Ch2, fpdc3, fpdc2tog, fpdc16, fpdc2tog, fpdc3, hdc1, fpdc17, sl st in first fpdc. (42)

**Rnd 30:** Ch2, fpdc2, fpdc2tog, fpdc16, fpdc2tog, fpdc2, hdc1, fpdc17, sl st in first fpdc. (40)

**Rnd 31:** Ch2, fpdc1, fpdc2tog, fpdc16, fpdc2tog, fpdc1, hdc1, fpdc17, sl st in first fpdc. (38)

**Rnd 32:** Ch2, fpdc2tog, fpdc16, fpdc2tog, hdc1, fpdc17, sl st in first fpdc. (36)

**Rnds 33-54:** Ch2, *fpdc3, bpdc3*, repeat * to * around, sl st in first fpdc. (36)

Fasten off and weave in ends.

## SIZE: 6-10 YEARS

**Rnd 1:** Start with a magic loop, ch2 (first ch2 doesn't count as first dc throughout the pattern), 6dc in the loop, sl st in first dc. (6)

**Rnd 2:** Ch2, 2fpdc in each stitch around, sl st in first fpdc. (12)

**Rnd 3:** Ch2, *fpdc1, 2fpdc in next st*, repeat * to * 2 more times, hdc1, 2fpdc in next st, repeat * to * 2 more times, sl st in first fpdc. (18)

**Rnd 4:** Ch2, *fpdc2, 2fpdc in next st*, repeat * to * 2 more times, hdc1, fpdc1, 2fpdc in next st, repeat * to * 2 more times, sl st in first fpdc. (24)

**Rnd 5:** Ch2, *fpdc3, 2fpdc in next st*, repeat * to * 2 more times, hdc1, fpdc2, 2fpdc in next st, repeat * to * 2 more times, sl st in first fpdc. (30)

**Rnd 6:** Ch2, *fpdc4, 2fpdc in next st*, repeat * to * 2 more times, hdc1, fpdc3, 2fpdc in next st, repeat * to * 2 more times, sl st in first fpdc. (36)

**Rnd 7:** Ch2, *fpdc5, 2fpdc in next st*, repeat * to * 2 more times, hdc1, fpdc4, 2fpdc in next st, repeat * to * 2 more times, sl st in first fpdc. (42)

**Rnds 8-27:** Ch2, fpdc21, hdc1, fpdc20, sl st in first fpdc. (42)

**Rnd 28:** Ch2, 2fpdc in next st, fpdc19, 2fpdc in next st, hdc1, fpdc20, sl st in first fpdc. (44)

**Rnd 29:** Ch2, fpdc1, 2fpdc in next st, fpdc19, 2fpdc in next st, fpdc1, hdc1, fpdc20, sl st in first fpdc. (46)

**Rnd 30:** Ch2, fpdc2, 2fpdc in next st, fpdc19, 2fpdc in next st, fpdc2, hdc1, fpdc20, sl st in first fpdc. (48)

**Rnd 31:** Ch2, fpdc3, 2fpdc in next st, fpdc19, 2fpdc in next st, fpdc3, hdc1, fpdc20, sl st in first fpdc. (50)

**Rnd 32:** Ch2, fpdc4, 2fpdc in next st, fpdc19, 2fpdc in next st, fpdc4, hdc1, fpdc20, sl st in first fpdc. (52)

**Rnd 33:** Ch2, fpdc5, 2fpdc in next st, fpdc19, 2fpdc in next st, fpdc5, hdc1, fpdc20, sl st in first fpdc. (54)

**Rnd 34:** Ch2, fpdc5, fpdc2tog, fpdc19, fpdc2tog, fpdc5, hdc1, fpdc20, sl st in first fpdc. (52)

**Rnd 35:** Ch2, fpdc4, fpdc2tog, fpdc19, fpdc2tog, fpdc4, hdc1, fpdc20, sl st in first fpdc. (50)

**Rnd 36:** Ch2, fpdc3, fpdc2tog, fpdc19, fpdc2tog, fpdc3, hdc1, fpdc20, sl st in first fpdc. (48)

**Rnd 37:** Ch2, fpdc2, fpdc2tog, fpdc19, fpdc2tog, fpdc2, hdc1, fpdc20, sl st in first fpdc. (46)

**Rnd 38:** Ch2, fpdc1, fpdc2tog, fpdc19, fpdc2tog, fpdc1, hdc1, fpdc20, sl st in first fpdc. (44)

**Rnd 39:** Ch2, fpdc2tog, fpdc19, fpdc2tog, hdc1, fpdc20, sl st in first fpdc. (42)

**Rnds 40-66:** Ch2, *fpdc3, bpdc3*, repeat * to * around, sl st in first fpdc. (42)

Fasten off and weave in ends.

**Rnd 1:** Start with a magic loop, ch2 (first ch2 doesn't count as first dc throughout the pattern), 6dc in the loop, sl st in first dc. (6)

**Rnd 2:** Ch2, 2fpdc in each stitch around, sl st in first fpdc. (12)

**Rnd 3:** Ch2, *fpdc1, 2fpdc in next st*, repeat * to * 2 more times, hdc1, 2fpdc in next st, repeat * to * 2 more times, sl st in first fpdc. (18)

**Rnd 4:** Ch2, *fpdc2, 2fpdc in next st*, repeat * to * 2 more times, hdc1, fpdc1, 2fpdc in next st, repeat * to * 2 more times, sl st in first fpdc. (24)

**Rnd 5:** Ch2, *fpdc3, 2fpdc in next st*, repeat * to * 2 more times, hdc1, fpdc2, 2fpdc in next st, repeat * to * 2 more times, sl st in first fpdc. (30)

**Rnd 6:** Ch2, *fpdc4, 2fpdc in next st*, repeat * to * 2 more times, hdc1, fpdc3, 2fpdc in next st, repeat * to * 2 more times, sl st in first fpdc. (36)

**Rnd 7:** Ch2, *fpdc5, 2fpdc in next st*, repeat * to * 2 more times, hdc1, fpdc4, 2fpdc in next st, repeat * to * 2 more times, sl st in first fpdc. (42)

**Rnd 8:** Ch2, *fpdc6, 2fpdc in next st*, repeat * to * 2 more times, hdc1, fpdc5, 2fpdc in next st, repeat * to * 2 more times, sl st in first fpdc. (48)

**Rnds 9-32:** Ch2, fpdc24, hdc1, fpdc23, sl st in first fpdc. (48)

**Rnd 33:** Ch2, 2fpdc in next st, fpdc22, 2fpdc in next st, hdc1, fpdc23, sl st in first fpdc. (50)

**Rnd 34:** Ch2, fpdc1, 2fpdc in next st, fpdc22, 2fpdc in next st, fpdc1, hdc1, fpdc23, sl st in first fpdc. (52)

**Rnd 35:** Ch2, fpdc2, 2fpdc in next st, fpdc22, 2fpdc in next st, fpdc2, hdc1, fpdc23, sl st in first fpdc. (54)

**Rnd 36:** Ch2, fpdc3, 2fpdc in next st, fpdc22, 2fpdc in next st, fpdc3, hdc1, fpdc23, sl st in first fpdc. (56)

**Rnd 37:** Ch2, fpdc4, 2fpdc in next st, fpdc22, 2fpdc in next st, fpdc4, hdc1, fpdc23, sl st in first fpdc. (58)

Rnd 38: Ch2, fpdc5, 2fpdc in next st, fpdc22, 2fpdc in next st, fpdc5, hdc1, fpdc23, sl st in first fpdc. (60)

Rnd 39: Ch2, fpdc6, 2fpdc in next st, fpdc22, 2fpdc in next st, fpdc6, hdc1, fpdc23, sl st in first fpdc. (62)

Rnd 40: Ch2, fpdc6, fpdc2tog, fpdc22, fpdc2tog, fpdc6, hdc1, fpdc23, sl st in first fpdc. (60)

Rnd 41: Ch2, fpdc5, fpdc2tog, fpdc22, fpdc2tog, fpdc5, hdc1, fpdc23, sl st in first fpdc. (58)

Rnd 42: Ch2, fpdc4, fpdc2tog, fpdc22, fpdc2tog, fpdc4, hdc1, fpdc23, sl st in first fpdc. (56)

Rnd 43: Ch2, fpdc3, fpdc2tog, fpdc22, fpdc2tog, fpdc3, hdc1, fpdc23, sl st in first fpdc. (54)

Rnd 44: Ch2, fpdc2, fpdc2tog, fpdc22, fpdc2tog, fpdc2, hdc1, fpdc23, sl st in first fpdc. (52)

Rnd 45: Ch2, fpdc1, fpdc2tog, fpdc22, fpdc2tog, fpdc1, hdc1, fpdc23, sl st in first fpdc. (50)

Rnd 46: Ch2, fpdc2tog, fpdc22, fpdc2tog, hdc1, fpdc23, sl st in first fpdc. (48)

Rnds 47–78: Ch2, *fpdc3, bpdc3*, repeat * to * around, sl st in first fpdc. (48)

Fasten off and weave in ends.

## SIZE: MEDIUM

Rnd 1: Start with a magic loop, ch2 (first ch2 doesn't count as first dc throughout the pattern), 6dc in the loop, sl st in first dc. (6)

Rnd 2: Ch2, 2fpdc in each stitch around, sl st in first fpdc. (12)

Rnd 3: Ch2, *fpdc1, 2fpdc in next st*, repeat * to * 2 more times, hdc1, 2fpdc in next st, repeat * to * 2 more times, sl st in first fpdc. (18)

Rnd 4: Ch2, *fpdc2, 2fpdc in next st*, repeat * to * 2 more times, hdc1, fpdc1, 2fpdc in next st, repeat * to * 2 more times, sl st in first fpdc. (24)

Rnd 5: Ch2, *fpdc3, 2fpdc in next st*, repeat * to * 2 more times, hdc1, fpdc2, 2fpdc in next st, repeat * to * 2 more times, sl st in first fpdc. (30)

Rnd 6: Ch2, *fpdc4, 2fpdc in next st*, repeat * to * 2 more times, hdc1, fpdc3, 2fpdc in next st, repeat * to * 2 more times, sl st in first fpdc. (36)

Rnd 7: Ch2, *fpdc5, 2fpdc in next st*, repeat * to * 2 more times, hdc1, fpdc4, 2fpdc in next st, repeat * to * 2 more times, sl st in first fpdc. (42)

Rnd 8: Ch2, *fpdc6, 2fpdc in next st*, repeat * to * 2 more times, hdc1, fpdc5, 2fpdc in next st, repeat * to * 2 more times, sl st in first fpdc. (48)

Rnd 9: Ch2, *fpdc7, 2fpdc in next st*, repeat * to * 2 more times, hdc1, fpdc6, 2fpdc in next st, repeat * to * 2 more times, sl st in first fpdc. (54)

Rnds 10–37: Ch2, fpdc27, hdc1, fpdc26, sl st in first fpdc. (54)

Rnd 38: Ch2, 2fpdc in next st, fpdc25, 2fpdc in next st, hdc1, fpdc26, sl st in first fpdc. (56)

Rnd 39: Ch2, fpdc1, 2fpdc in next st, fpdc25, 2fpdc in next st, fpdc1, hdc1, fpdc26, sl st in first fpdc. (58)

Rnd 40: Ch2, fpdc2, 2fpdc in next st, fpdc25, 2fpdc in next st, fpdc2, hdc1, fpdc26, sl st in first fpdc. (60)

Rnd 41: Ch2, fpdc3, 2fpdc in next st, fpdc25, 2fpdc in next st, fpdc3, hdc1, fpdc26, sl st in first fpdc. (62)

Rnd 42: Ch2, fpdc4, 2fpdc in next st, fpdc25, 2fpdc in next st, fpdc4, hdc1, fpdc26, sl st in first fpdc. (64)

Rnd 43: Ch2, fpdc5, 2fpdc in next st, fpdc25, 2fpdc in next st, fpdc5, hdc1, fpdc26, sl st in first fpdc. (66)

Rnd 44: Ch2, fpdc6, 2fpdc in next st, fpdc25, 2fpdc in next st, fpdc6, hdc1, fpdc26, sl st in first fpdc. (68)

Rnd 45: Ch2, fpdc7, 2fpdc in next st, fpdc25, 2fpdc in next st, fpdc7, hdc1, fpdc26, sl st in first fpdc. (70)

Rnd 46: Ch2, fpdc7, fpdc2tog, fpdc25, fpdc2tog, fpdc7, hdc1, fpdc26, sl st in first fpdc. (68)

Rnd 47: Ch2, fpdc6, fpdc2tog, fpdc25, fpdc2tog, fpdc6, hdc1, fpdc26, sl st in first fpdc. (66)

Rnd 48: Ch2, fpdc5, fpdc2tog, fpdc25, fpdc2tog, fpdc5, hdc1, fpdc26, sl st in first fpdc. (64)

Rnd 49: Ch2, fpdc4, fpdc2tog, fpdc25, fpdc2tog, fpdc4, hdc1, fpdc26, sl st in first fpdc. (62)

Rnd 50: Ch2, fpdc3, fpdc2tog, fpdc25, fpdc2tog, fpdc3, hdc1, fpdc26, sl st in first fpdc. (60)

Rnd 51: Ch2, fpdc2, fpdc2tog, fpdc25, fpdc2tog, fpdc2, hdc1, fpdc26, sl st in first fpdc. (58)

Rnd 52: Ch2, fpdc1, fpdc2tog, fpdc25, fpdc2tog, fpdc1, hdc1, fpdc26, sl st in first fpdc. (56)

**Rnd 53:** Ch2, fpdc2tog, fpdc25, fpdc2tog, hdc1, fpdc26, sl st in first fpdc. (54)

**Rnds 54-90:** Ch2, *fpdc3, bpdc3*, repeat * to * around, sl st in first fpdc. (54)

Fasten off and weave in ends.

## SIZE: LARGE

---

**Rnd 1:** Start with a magic loop, ch2 (first ch2 doesn't count as first dc throughout the pattern), 6dc in the loop, sl st in first dc. (6)

**Rnd 2:** Ch2, 2fpdc in each stitch around, sl st in first fpdc. (12)

**Rnd 3:** Ch2, *fpdc1, 2fpdc in next st*, repeat * to * 2 more times, hdc1, 2fpdc in next st, repeat * to * 2 more times, sl st in first fpdc. (18)

**Rnd 4:** Ch2, *fpdc2, 2fpdc in next st*, repeat * to * 2 more times, hdc1, fpdc1, 2fpdc in next st, repeat * to * 2 more times, sl st in first fpdc. (24)

**Rnd 5:** Ch2, *fpdc3, 2fpdc in next st*, repeat * to * 2 more times, hdc1, fpdc2, 2fpdc in next st, repeat * to * 2 more times, sl sl in first fpdc. (30)

**Rnd 6:** Ch2, *fpdc4, 2fpdc in next st*, repeat * to * 2 more times, hdc1, fpdc3, 2fpdc in next st, repeat * to * 2 more times, sl st in first fpdc. (36)

**Rnd 7:** Ch2, *fpdc5, 2fpdc in next st*, repeat * to * 2 more times, hdc1, fpdc4, 2fpdc in next st, repeat * to * 2 more times, sl st in first fpdc. (42)

**Rnd 8:** Ch2, *fpdc6, 2fpdc in next st*, repeat * to * 2 more times, hdc1, fpdc5, 2fpdc in next st, repeat * to * 2 more times, sl st in first fpdc. (48)

**Rnd 9:** Ch2, *fpdc7, 2fpdc in next st*, repeat * to * 2 more times, hdc1, fpdc6, 2fpdc in next st, repeat * to * 2 more times, sl st in first fpdc. (54)

**Rnd 10:** Ch2, *fpdc8, 2fpdc in next st*, repeat * to * 2 more times, hdc1, fpdc7, 2fpdc in next st, repeat * to * 2 more times, sl st in first fpdc. (60)

**Rnds 11-42:** Ch2, fpdc30, hdc1, fpdc29, sl st in first fpdc. (60)

**Rnd 43:** Ch2, 2fpdc in next st, fpdc28, 2fpdc in next st, hdc1, fpdc29, sl st in first fpdc. (62)

**Rnd 44:** Ch2, fpdc1, 2fpdc in next st, fpdc28, 2fpdc in next st, fpdc1, hdc1, fpdc29, sl st in first fpdc. (64)

**Rnd 45:** Ch2, fpdc2, 2fpdc in next st, fpdc28, 2fpdc in next st, fpdc2, hdc1, fpdc29, sl st in first fpdc. (66)

**Rnd 46:** Ch2, fpdc3, 2fpdc in next st, fpdc28, 2fpdc in next st, fpdc3, hdc1, fpdc29, sl st in first fpdc. (68)

**Rnd 47:** Ch2, fpdc4, 2fpdc in next st, fpdc28, 2fpdc in next st, fpdc4, hdc1, fpdc29, sl st in first fpdc. (70)

**Rnd 48:** Ch2, fpdc5, 2fpdc in next st, fpdc28, 2fpdc in next st, fpdc5, hdc1, fpdc20, sl st in first fpdc. (72)

**Rnd 49:** Ch2, fpdc6, 2fpdc in next st, fpdc28, 2fpdc in next st, fpdc6, hdc1, fpdc29, sl st in first fpdc. (74)

**Rnd 50:** Ch2, fpdc7, 2fpdc in next st, fpdc28, 2fpdc in next st, fpdc7, hdc1, fpdc29, sl st in first fpdc. (76)

**Rnd 51:** Ch2, fpdc8, 2fpdc in next st, fpdc28, 2fpdc in next st, fpdc8, hdc1, fpdc29, sl st in first fpdc. (78)

**Rnd 52:** Ch2, fpdc8, fpdc2tog, fpdc28, fpdc2tog, fpdc8, hdc1, fpdc29, sl st in first fpdc. (76)

**Rnd 53:** Ch2, fpdc7, fpdc2tog, fpdc28, fpdc2tog, fpdc7, hdc1, fpdc29, sl st in first fpdc. (74)

**Rnd 54:** Ch2, fpdc6, fpdc2tog, fpdc28, fpdc2tog, fpdc6, hdc1, fpdc29, sl st in first fpdc. (72)

**Rnd 55:** Ch2, fpdc5, fpdc2tog, fpdc28, fpdc2tog, fpdc5, hdc1, fpdc29, sl st in first fpdc. (70)

**Rnd 56:** Ch2, fpdc4, fpdc2tog, fpdc28, fpdc2tog, fpdc4, hdc1, fpdc29, sl st in first fpdc. (68)

**Rnd 57:** Ch2, fpdc3, fpdc2tog, fpdc28, fpdc2tog, fpdc3, hdc1, fpdc29, sl st in first fpdc. (66)

**Rnd 58:** Ch2, fpdc2, fpdc2tog, fpdc28, fpdc2tog, fpdc2, hdc1, fpdc29, sl st in first fpdc. (64)

**Rnd 59:** Ch2, fpdc1, fpdc2tog, fpdc28, fpdc2tog, fpdc1, hdc1, fpdc29, sl st in first fpdc. (62)

**Rnd 60:** Ch2, fpdc2tog, fpdc28, fpdc2tog, hdc1, fpdc29, sl st in first fpdc. (60)

**Rnds 61-102:** Ch2, *fpdc1, bpdc1*, repeat * to * around, sl st in first fpdc. (60)

Fasten off and weave in ends.

# honeycomb

THE HONEYCOMB SOCKS ARE THE MOST DIFFICULT PATTERN
IN THIS BOOK, BUT YOUR EFFORTS WILL BE REWARDED
WITH A GORGEOUS PAIR OF SOCKS.

For help in choosing the right size, see page 15.
For help in choosing the right hook size and checking gauge, see page 16.

## MATERIALS

**Yarn**

**Orange socks:** Sheepjes Metropolis, #1 super fine weight (75% wool, 25% nylon; 218.7 yd./200 m per 1.75 oz./50 g); color #075

**Yellow socks:** Durable Soqs, #1 super fine weight (75% wool, 25% polyamide; 230 yd./210 m per 1.76 oz./50 g); color #411

**Hook**
US size G-6 (4 mm)

**Gauge**
5 fpdc wide and 4 rnds high = 0.7 in./2 cm

**Estimated total yarn required**
12–24 months: 230 yd./210 m; 3–5 years: 460 yd./420 m; 6–10 years: 460 yd./420 m; Small: 689 yd./630 m; Medium: 689 yd./630 m

## ABBREVIATIONS

| | | |
|---|---|---|
| ⌒ | **ch** | chain |
| ┼ | **dc** | double crochet |
| ● | **sl st** | slip stitch |
| ┬ | **hdc** | half double crochet |
| ╪ | **bpdc** | back post double crochet |
| ╪ | **fpdc** | front post double crochet |
| ╪ | **fptrc** | front post triple crochet |
| ⅄ | **fpdc2tog** | front post double crochet 2 together (1 stitch decreased) |
| Ⅴ | **2 fpdc in the next stitch** | 2 fpdc in the same stitch (1 stitch increased) |

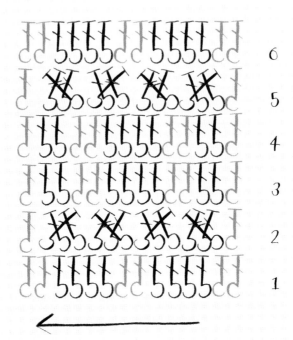

6

5

4

3

2

1

**SIZE: 12-24 MONTHS**

---

**HONEYCOMB 12-24 MOTIF 1:** Bpdc2, fpdc4, bpdc2, fpdc4, bpdc2.

**HONEYCOMB 12-24 MOTIF 2:** Bpdc1, *skip 1 stitch, fpdc2, make 1 fptrc in the stitch you just skipped but behind the 2 previous fpdc, skip 2 stitches, fptrc1, make 1 fpdc in each of the 2 stitches you just skipped but in front of the previous fptrc*, repeat from * to * 1 more time, bpdc1.

**HONEYCOMB 12-24 MOTIF 3-4:** Bpdc1, fpdc2, bpdc2, fpdc4, bpdc2, fpdc2, bpdc1.

**HONEYCOMB 12-24 MOTIF 5:** Bpdc1, *skip 2 stitches, fptrc1, make 1 fpdc in each of the 2 stitches you just skipped but in front of the previous fptrc, skip 1 stitch, fpdc2, make 1 fptrc in the stitch you just skipped but behind the 2 previous fpdc*, repeat from * to * 1 more time, bpdc1.

**HONEYCOMB 12-24 MOTIF 6:** Just like honeycomb 12-24 motif 1.

Rnd 1:    Start with a magic loop, ch2 (first ch2 doesn't count as first dc throughout the pattern), 6dc in the loop, sl st in first dc. (6)

Rnd 2:    Ch2, 2fpdc in each stitch around, sl st in first fpdc. (12)

Rnd 3:    Ch2, *fpdc1, 2fpdc in next st*, repeat * to * 2 more times, hdc1, 2fpdc in next st, repeat * to * 2 more times, sl st in first fpdc. (18)

Rnd 4:    Ch2, *fpdc2, 2fpdc in next st*, repeat * to * 2 more times, hdc1, fpdc1, 2fpdc in next st, repeat * to * 2 more times, sl st in first fpdc. (24)

Rnd 5:    Ch2, *fpdc3, 2fpdc in next st*, repeat * to * 2 more times, hdc1, fpdc2, 2fpdc in next st, repeat * to * 2 more times, sl st in first fpdc. (30)

Rnd 6:    Ch2, fpdc15, hdc1, honeycomb 12-24 motif 1, sl st in first fpdc. (30)

Rnd 7:    Ch2, fpdc15, hdc1, honeycomb 12-24 motif 2, sl st in first fpdc. (30)

Rnds 8-9: Ch2, fpdc15, hdc1, honeycomb 12-24 motif 3-4, sl st in first fpdc. (30)

Rnd 10: Ch2, fpdc15, hdc1, honeycomb 12-24 motif 5, sl st in first fpdc. (30)

Rnd 11: Ch2, fpdc15, hdc1, honeycomb 12-24 motif 6, sl st in first fpdc. (30)

Rnds 12-17: Repeat Rnds 6-11.

**Rnd 18:** Ch2, 2fpdc in next st, fpdc13, 2fpdc in next st, hdc1, honeycomb 12-24 motif 1, sl st in first fpdc. (32)

**Rnd 19:** Ch2, fpdc1, 2fpdc in next st, fpdc13, 2fpdc in next st, fpdc1, hdc1, honeycomb 12-24 motif 2, sl st in first fpdc. (34)

**Rnd 20:** Ch2, fpdc2, 2fpdc in next st, fpdc13, 2fpdc in next st, fpdc2, hdc1, honeycomb 12-24 motif 3, sl st in first fpdc. (36)

**Rnd 21:** Ch2, fpdc3, 2fpdc in next st, fpdc13, 2fpdc in next st, fpdc3, hdc1, honeycomb 12-24 motif 4, sl st in first fpdc. (38)

**Rnd 22:** Ch2, fpdc3, fpdc2tog, fpdc13, fpdc2tog, fpdc3, hdc1, honeycomb 12-24 motif 5, sl st in first fpdc. (36)

**Rnd 23:** Ch2, fpdc2, fpdc2tog, fpdc13, fpdc2tog, fpdc2, hdc1, honeycomb 12-24 motif 6, sl st in first fpdc. (34)

**Rnd 24:** Ch2, fpdc1, fpdc2tog, fpdc13, fpdc2tog, fpdc1, hdc1, honeycomb 12-24 motif 1, sl st in first fpdc. (32)

**Rnd 25:** Ch2, fpdc2tog, fpdc13, fpdc2tog, hdc1, honeycomb 12-24 motif 2, sl st in first fpdc. (30)

**Rnd 26-27:** Ch2, bpdc1, honeycomb 12-24 motif 3-4, bpdc1, honeycomb 12-24 motif 3-4, sl st in first bpdc. (30)

**Rnd 28:** Ch2, bpdc1, honeycomb 12-24 motif 5, bpdc1, honeycomb 12-24 motif 5, sl st in first bpdc. (30)

**Rnd 29:** Ch2, bpdc1, honeycomb 12-24 motif 6, bpdc1, honeycomb 12-24 motif 6, sl st in first bpdc. (30)

**Rnd 30:** Ch2, bpdc1, honeycomb 12-24 motif 1, bpdc1, honeycomb 12-24 motif 1, sl st in first bpdc. (30)

**Rnd 31:** Ch2, bpdc1, honeycomb 12-24 motif 2, bpdc1, honeycomb 12-24 motif 2, sl st in first bpdc. (30)

**Rnd 32:** Ch2, bpdc1, honeycomb 12-24 motif 3, bpdc1, honeycomb 12-24 motif 3, sl st in first bpdc. (30)

**Rnd 33:** Ch2, fpdc1 in each stitch around, sl st in first fpdc. (30)

**Rnds 34-35:** Ch2, *fpdc1, bpdc1*, repeat * to * around, sl st in first fpdc. (30)

Fasten off and weave in ends.

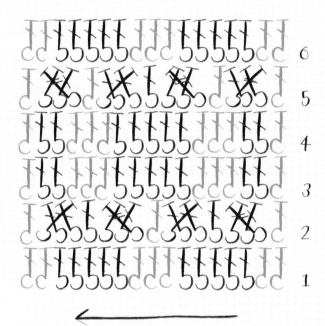

6
5
4
3
2
1

**SIZE: 3-5 YEARS**

**HONEYCOMB 3-5 MOTIF 1:** Bpdc2, fpdc5, bpdc3, fpdc5, bpdc2.

**HONEYCOMB 3-5 MOTIF 2:** Bpdc1, *skip 1 stitch, fpdc2, make 1 fptrc in the stitch you just skipped but behind the 2 previous fpdc, fpdc1, skip 2 stitches, fptrc1, make 1 fpdc in each of the 2 stitches you just skipped but in front of the previous fptrc*, bpdc1, repeat from * to * 1 more time, bpdc1.

**HONEYCOMB 3-5 MOTIF 3-4:** Bpdc1, fpdc2, bpdc3, fpdc5, bpdc3, fpdc2, bpdc1.

**HONEYCOMB 3-5 MOTIF 5:** Bpdc1, *skip 2 stitches, fptrc1, make 1 fpdc in each of the 2 stitches you just skipped but in front of the previous fptrc, bpdc1, skip 1 stitch, fpdc2, make 1 fptrc in the stitch you just skipped but behind the 2 previous fpdc*, fpdc1, repeat from * to * 1 more time, bpdc1.

**HONEYCOMB 3-5 MOTIF 6:** Just like honeycomb 3-5 motif 1.

Rnd 1:   Start with a magic loop, ch2 (first ch2 doesn't count as first dc throughout the pattern), 6dc in the loop, sl st in first dc. (6)

**Rnd 2:** Ch2, 2fpdc in each stitch around, sl st in first fpdc. (12)

**Rnd 3:** Ch2, *fpdc1, 2fpdc in next st*, repeat * to * 2 more times, hdc1, 2fpdc in next st, repeat * to * 2 more times, sl st in first fpdc. (18)

**Rnd 4:** Ch2, *fpdc2, 2fpdc in next st*, repeat * to * 2 more times, hdc1, fpdc1, 2fpdc in next st, repeat * to * 2 more times, sl st in first fpdc. (24)

**Rnd 5:** Ch2, *fpdc3, 2fpdc in next st*, repeat * to * 2 more times, hdc1, fpdc2, 2fpdc in next st, repeat * to * 2 more times, sl st in first fpdc. (30)

**Rnd 6:** Ch2, *fpdc4, 2fpdc in next st*, repeat * to * 2 more times, hdc1, fpdc3, 2fpdc in next st, repeat * to * 2 more times, sl st in first fpdc. (36)

**Rnd 7:** Ch2, fpdc18, hdc1, honeycomb 3-5 motif 1, sl st in first fpdc. (36)

**Rnd 8:** Ch2, fpdc18, hdc1, honeycomb 3-5 motif 2, sl st in first fpdc. (36)

**Rnds 9-10:** Ch2, fpdc18, hdc1, honeycomb 3-5 motif 3-4, sl st in first fpdc. (36)

**Rnd 11:** Ch2, fpdc18, hdc1, honeycomb 3-5 motif 5, sl st in first fpdc. (36)

**Rnd 12:** Ch2, fpdc18, hdc1, honeycomb 3-5 motif 6, sl st in first fpdc. (36)

**Rnds 13-21:** Repeat Rnds 7-12; you'll end with Rnd 9.

**Rnd 22:** Ch2, fpdc18, hdc1, honeycomb 3-5 motif 4, sl st in first fpdc. (36)

**Rnd 23:** Ch2, 2fpdc in next st, fpdc16, 2fpdc in next st, hdc1, honeycomb 3-5 motif 5, sl st in first fpdc. (38)

**Rnd 24:** Ch2, fpdc1, 2fpdc in next st, fpdc16, 2fpdc in next st, fpdc1, hdc1, honeycomb 3-5 motif 6 sl st in first fpdc. (40)

**Rnd 25:** Ch2, fpdc2, 2fpdc in next st, fpdc16, 2fpdc in next st, fpdc2, hdc1, honeycomb 3-5 motif 1, sl st in first fpdc. (42)

**Rnd 26:** Ch2, fpdc3, 2fpdc in next st, fpdc16, 2fpdc in next st, fpdc3, hdc1, honeycomb 3-5 motif 2, sl st in first fpdc. (44)

**Rnd 27:** Ch2, fpdc4, 2fpdc in next st, fpdc16, 2fpdc in next st, fpdc4, hdc1, honeycomb 3-5 motif 3, sl st in first fpdc. (46)

**Rnd 28:** Ch2, fpdc4, fpdc2tog, fpdc16, fpdc2tog, fpdc4, hdc1, honeycomb 3-5 motif 4, sl st in first fpdc. (44)

**Rnd 29:** Ch2, fpdc3, fpdc2tog, fpdc16, fpdc2tog, fpdc3, hdc1, honeycomb 3-5 motif 5, sl st in first fpdc. (42)

**Rnd 30:** Ch2, fpdc2, fpdc2tog, fpdc16, fpdc2tog, fpdc2, hdc1, honeycomb 3-5 motif 6, sl st in first fpdc. (40)

**Rnd 31:** Ch2, fpdc1, fpdc2tog, fpdc16, fpdc2tog, fpdc1, hdc1, honeycomb 3-5 motif 1, sl st in first fpdc. (38)

**Rnd 32:** Ch2, fpdc2tog, fpdc16, fpdc2tog, hdc1, honeycomb 3-5 motif 2, sl st in first fpdc. (36)

**Rnds 33-34:** Ch2, bpdc1, honeycomb 3-5 motif 3-4, hdc1, honeycomb 3-5 motif 3-4, sl st in first bpdc. (36)

**Rnd 35:** Ch2, bpdc1, honeycomb 3-5 motif 5, bpdc1, honeycomb 3-5 motif 5, sl st in first bpdc. (36)

**Rnd 36:** Ch2, bpdc1, honeycomb 3-5 motif 6, bpdc1, honeycomb 3-5 motif 6, sl st in first bpdc. (36)

**Rnd 37:** Ch2, bpdc1, honeycomb 3-5 motif 1, bpdc1, honeycomb 3-5 motif 1, sl st in first bpdc. (36)

**Rnd 38:** Ch2, bpdc1, honeycomb 3-5 motif 2, bpdc1, honeycomb 3-5 motif 2, sl st in first bpdc. (36)

**Rnd 39:** Ch2, bpdc1, honeycomb 3-5 motif 3, bpdc1, honeycomb 3-5 motif 3, sl st in first bpdc. (36)

**Rnd 40:** Ch2, fpdc1 in each stitch around, sl st in first fpdc. (36)

**Rnds 41-44:** Ch2, *fpdc1, bpdc1*, repeat * to * around, sl st in first fpdc. (36)

Fasten off and weave in ends.

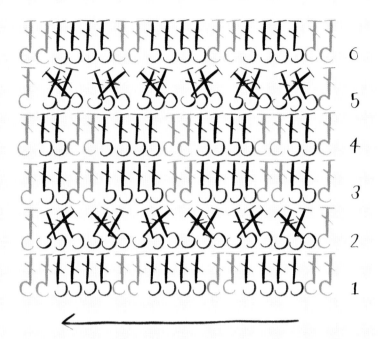

6
5
4
3
2
1

**SIZE: 6-10 YEARS**

---

**HONEYCOMB 6-10 MOTIF 1:** Bpdc2, *fpdc4, bpdc2*, repeat * to * 2 more times.

**HONEYCOMB 6-10 MOTIF 2:** Bpdc1, *skip 1 stitch, fpdc2, make 1 fptrc in the stitch you just skipped but behind the 2 previous fpdc, skip 2 stitches, fptrc1, make 1 fpdc in each of the 2 stitches you just skipped but in front of the previous fptrc*, repeat from * to * 2 more times, bpdc1.

**HONEYCOMB 6-10 MOTIF 3-4:** Bpdc1, fpdc2, bpdc2, fpdc4, bpdc2, fpdc4, bpdc2, fpdc2, bpdc1.

**HONEYCOMB 6-10 MOTIF 5:** Bpdc1, *skip 2 stitches, fptrc1, make 1 fpdc in each of the 2 stitches you just skipped but in front of the previous fptrc, skip 1 stitch, fpdc2, make 1 fptrc in the stitch you just skipped but behind the 2 previous fpdc, repeat from * to * 2 more times, bpdc1.

**HONEYCOMB 6-10 MOTIF 6:** Just like Honeycomb 6-10 motif 1.

Rnd 1:  Start with a magic loop, ch2 (first ch2 doesn't count as first dc throughout the pattern), 6dc in the loop, sl st in first dc. (6)

Rnd 2:  Ch2, 2fpdc in each stitch around, sl st in first fpdc. (12)

Rnd 3:  Ch2, *fpdc1, 2fpdc in next st*, repeat * to * 2 more times, hdc1, 2fpdc in next st, repeat * to * 2 more times, sl st in first fpdc. (18)

Rnd 4:  Ch2, *fpdc2, 2fpdc in next st*, repeat * to * 2 more times, hdc1, fpdc1, 2fpdc in next st, repeat * to * 2 more times, sl st in first fpdc. (24)

Rnd 5:  Ch2, *fpdc3, 2fpdc in next st*, repeat * to * 2 more times, hdc1, fpdc2, 2fpdc in next st, repeat * to * 2 more times, sl st in first fpdc. (30)

Rnd 6:  Ch2, *fpdc4, 2fpdc in next st*, repeat * to * 2 more times, hdc1, fpdc3, 2fpdc in next st, repeat * to * 2 more times, sl st in first fpdc. (36)

Rnd 7:  Ch2, *fpdc5, 2fpdc in next st*, repeat * to * 2 more times, hdc1, fpdc4, 2fpdc in next st, repeat * to * 2 more times, sl st in first fpdc. (42)

Rnd 8:  Ch2, fpdc21, hdc1, honeycomb 6-10 motif 1, sl st in first fpdc. (42)

Rnd 9:  Ch2, fpdc21, hdc1, honeycomb 6-10 motif 2, sl st in first fpdc. (42)

**Rnds 10–11:** Ch2, fpdc21, hdc1, honeycomb 6–10 motif 3–4, sl st in first fpdc. (42)

**Rnd 12:** Ch2, fpdc21, hdc1, honeycomb 6–10 motif 5, sl st in first fpdc. (42)

**Rnd 13:** Ch2, fpdc21, hdc1, honeycomb 6–10 motif 6, sl st in first fpdc. (42)

**Rnds 14–27:** Repeat Rnds 8–13; you'll end with Rnd 9.

**Rnd 28:** Ch2, fpdc21, hdc1, honeycomb 6–10 motif 3, sl st in first fpdc. (42)

**Rnd 29:** Ch2, 2fpdc in next st, fpdc19, 2fpdc in next st, hdc1, honeycomb 6–10 motif 4, sl st in first fpdc. (44)

**Rnd 30:** Ch2, fpdc1, 2fpdc in next st, fpdc19, 2fpdc in next st, fpdc1, hdc1, honeycomb 6–10 motif 5, sl st in first fpdc. (46)

**Rnd 31:** Ch2, fpdc2, 2fpdc in next st, fpdc19, 2fpdc in next st, fpdc2, hdc1, honeycomb 6–10 motif 6, sl st in first fpdc. (48)

**Rnd 32:** Ch2, fpdc3, 2fpdc in next st, fpdc19, 2fpdc in next st, fpdc3, hdc1, honeycomb 6–10 motif 1, sl st in first fpdc. (50)

**Rnd 33:** Ch2, fpdc4, 2fpdc in next st, fpdc19, 2fpdc in next st, fpdc4, hdc1, honeycomb 6–10 motif 2, sl st in first fpdc. (52)

**Rnd 34:** Ch2, fpdc5, 2fpdc in next st, fpdc19, 2fpdc in next st, fpdc5, hdc1, honeycomb 6–10 motif 3, sl st in first fpdc. (54)

**Rnd 35:** Ch2, fpdc5, fpdc2tog, fpdc19, fpdc2tog, fpdc5, hdc1, honeycomb 6–10 motif 4, sl st in first fpdc. (52)

**Rnd 36:** Ch2, fpdc4, fpdc2tog, fpdc19, fpdc2tog, fpdc4, hdc1, honeycomb 6–10 motif 5, sl st in first fpdc. (50)

**Rnd 37:** Ch2, fpdc3, fpdc2tog, fpdc19, fpdc2tog, fpdc3, hdc1, honeycomb 6–10 motif 6, sl st in first fpdc. (48)

**Rnd 38:** Ch2, fpdc2, fpdc2tog, fpdc19, fpdc2tog, fpdc2, hdc1, honeycomb 6–10 motif 1, sl st in first fpdc. (46)

**Rnd 39:** Ch2, fpdc1, fpdc2tog, fpdc19, fpdc2tog, fpdc1, hdc1, honeycomb 6–10 motif 2, sl st in first fpdc. (44)

**Rnd 40:** Ch2, fpdc2tog, fpdc19, fpdc2tog, hdc1, honeycomb 6–10 motif 3, sl st in first fpdc. (42)

**Rnd 41:** Ch2, bpdc1, honeycomb 6–10 motif 4, bpdc1, honeycomb 6–10 motif 4, sl st in first bpdc. (42)

**Rnd 42:** Ch2, bpdc1, honeycomb 6–10 motif 5, bpdc1, honeycomb 6–10 motif 5, sl st in first bpdc. (42)

**Rnd 43:** Ch2, bpdc1, honeycomb 6–10 motif 6, bpdc1, honeycomb 6–10 motif 6, sl st in first bpdc. (42)

**Rnd 44:** Ch2, bpdc1, honeycomb 6–10 motif 1, bpdc1, honeycomb 6–10 motif 1, sl st in first bpdc. (42)

**Rnd 45:** Ch2, bpdc1, honeycomb 6–10 motif 2, bpdc1, honeycomb 6–10 motif 2, sl st in first bpdc. (42)

**Rnds 46–47:** Ch2, bpdc1, honeycomb 6–10 motif 3–4, bpdc1, honeycomb 6–10 motif 3–4, sl st in first bpdc. (42)

**Rnd 48:** Ch2, bpdc1, honeycomb 6–10 motif 5, bpdc1, honeycomb 6–10 motif 5, sl st in first bpdc. (42)

**Rnd 49:** Ch2, bpdc1, honeycomb 6–10 motif 6, bpdc1, honeycomb 6–10 motif 6, sl st in first bpdc. (42)

**Rnd 50:** Ch2, fpdc1 in each stitch around, sl st in first fpdc. (42)

**Rnds 51–54:** Ch2, *fpdc1, bpdc1*, repeat * to * around, sl st in first fpdc. (42)

Fasten off and weave in ends.

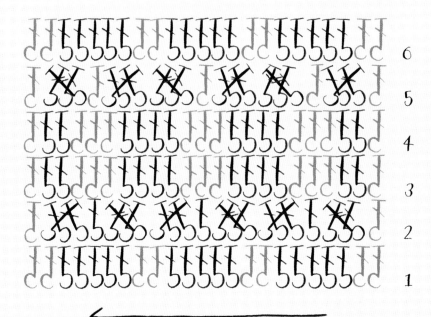

6

5

4

3

2

1

**SIZE: SMALL**

**HONEYCOMB SMALL MOTIF 1:** Bpdc2, *fpdc5, bpdc2*, repeat * to * 2 more times.

**HONEYCOMB SMALL MOTIF 2:** Bpdc1, *skip 1 stitch, fpdc2, make 1 fptrc in the stitch you just skipped but behind the 2 previous fpdc, fpdc1, skip 2 stitches, fptrc1, make 1 fpdc in each of the 2 stitches you just skipped but in front of the previous fptrc*, repeat from * to * 2 more times, bpdc1.

**HONEYCOMB SMALL MOTIF 3-4:** Bpdc1, fpdc2, bpdc3, fpdc4, bpdc3, fpdc4, bpdc3, fpdc2, bpdc1.

**HONEYCOMB SMALL MOTIF 5:** Bpdc1, *skip 2 stitches, fptrc1, make 1 fpdc in each of the 2 stitches you just skipped but in front of the previous fptrc, bpdc1, skip 1 stitch, fpdc2, make 1 fptrc in the stitch you just skipped but behind the 2 previous fpdc*, repeat from * to * 2 more times, bpdc1.

**HONEYCOMB SMALL MOTIF 6:** Just like Honeycomb Small motif 1.

**Rnd 1:** Start with a magic loop, ch2 (first ch2 doesn't count as first dc throughout the pattern), 6dc in the loop, sl st in first dc. (6)

**Rnd 2:** Ch2, 2fpdc in each stitch around, sl st in first fpdc. (12)

**Rnd 3:** Ch2, *fpdc1, 2fpdc in next st*, repeat * to * 2 more times, hdc1, 2fpdc in next st, repeat * to * 2 more times, sl st in first fpdc. (18)

**Rnd 4:** Ch2, *fpdc2, 2fpdc in next st*, repeat to * 2 more times, hdc1, fpdc1, 2fpdc in next st, repeat * to * 2 more times, sl st in first fpdc. (24)

**Rnd 5:** Ch2, *fpdc3, 2fpdc in next st*, repeat * to * 2 more times, hdc1, fpdc2, 2fpdc in next st, repeat * to * 2 more times, sl st in first fpdc. (30)

**Rnd 6:** Ch2, *fpdc4, 2fpdc in next st*, repeat * to * 2 more times, hdc1, fpdc3, 2fpdc in next st, repeat * to * 2 more times, sl st in first fpdc. (36)

**Rnd 7:** Ch2, *fpdc5, 2fpdc in next st*, repeat * to * 2 more times, hdc1, fpdc4, 2fpdc in next st, repeat * to * 2 more times, sl st in first fpdc. (42)

**Rnd 8:** Ch2, *fpdc6, 2fpdc in next st*, repeat * to * 2 more times, hdc1, fpdc5, 2fpdc in next st, repeat * to * 2 more times, sl st in first fpdc. (48)

Rnd 9:  Ch2, fpdc24, hdc1, honeycomb Small motif 1, sl st in first fpdc. (48)

Rnd 10: Ch2, fpdc24, hdc1, honeycomb Small motif 2, sl st in first fpdc. (48)

Rnds 11-12: Ch2, fpdc24, hdc1, honeycomb Small motif 3-4, sl st in first fpdc. (48)

Rnd 13: Ch2, fpdc24, hdc1, honeycomb Small motif 5, sl st in first fpdc. (48)

Rnd 14: Ch2, fpdc24, hdc1, honeycomb Small motif 6, sl st in first fpdc. (48)

Rnds 15-32: Repeat Rnds 9-14.

Rnd 33: Ch2, 2fpdc in next st, fpdc22, 2fpdc in next st, hdc1, honeycomb Small motif 1, sl st in first fpdc. (50)

Rnd 34: Ch2, fpdc1, 2fpdc in next st, fpdc22, 2fpdc in next st, fpdc1, hdc1, honeycomb Small motif 2, sl st in first fpdc. (52)

Rnd 35: Ch2, fpdc2, 2fpdc in next st, fpdc22, 2fpdc in next st, fpdc2, hdc1, honeycomb Small motif 3, sl st in first fpdc. (54)

Rnd 36: Ch2, fpdc3, 2fpdc in next st, fpdc22, 2fpdc in next st, fpdc3, hdc1, honeycomb Small motif 4, sl st in first fpdc. (56)

Rnd 37: Ch2, fpdc4, 2fpdc in next st, fpdc22, 2fpdc in next st, fpdc4, hdc1, honeycomb Small motif 5, sl st in first fpdc. (58)

Rnd 38: Ch2, fpdc5, 2fpdc in next st, fpdc22, 2fpdc in next st, fpdc5, hdc1, honeycomb Small motif 6, sl st in first fpdc. (60)

Rnd 39: Ch2, fpdc6, 2fpdc in next st, fpdc22, 2fpdc in next st, fpdc6, hdc1, honeycomb Small motif 1, sl st in first fpdc. (62)

Rnd 40: Ch2, fpdc6, fpdc2tog, fpdc22, fpdc2tog, fpdc6, hdc1, honeycomb Small motif 2, sl st in first fpdc. (60)

Rnd 41: Ch2, fpdc5, fpdc2tog, fpdc22, fpdc2tog, fpdc5, hdc1, honeycomb Small motif 3, sl st in first fpdc. (58)

Rnd 42: Ch2, fpdc4, fpdc2tog, fpdc22, fpdc2tog, fpdc4, hdc1, honeycomb Small motif 4, sl st in first fpdc. (56)

Rnd 43: Ch2, fpdc3, fpdc2tog, fpdc22, fpdc2tog, fpdc3, hdc1, honeycomb Small motif 5, sl st in first fpdc. (54)

Rnd 44: Ch2, fpdc2, fpdc2tog, fpdc22, fpdc2tog, fpdc2, hdc1, honeycomb Small motif 6, sl st in first fpdc. (52)

Rnd 45: Ch2, fpdc1, fpdc2tog, fpdc22, fpdc2tog, fpdc1, hdc1, honeycomb Small motif 1, sl st in first fpdc. (50)

Rnd 46: Ch2, fpdc2tog, fpdc22, fpdc2tog, hdc1, honeycomb Small motif 2, sl st in first fpdc (48)

Rnds 47-48: Ch2, bpdc1, honeycomb Small motif 3-4, bpdc1, honeycomb Small motif 3-4, sl st in first bpdc. (48)

Rnd 49: Ch2, bpdc1, honeycomb Small motif 5, bpdc1, honeycomb Small motif 5, sl st in first bpdc. (48)

Rnd 50: Ch2, bpdc1, honeycomb Small motif 6, bpdc1, honeycomb Small motif 6, sl st in first bpdc. (48)

Rnd 51: Ch2, bpdc1, honeycomb Small motif 1, bpdc1, honeycomb Small motif 1, sl st in first bpdc. (48)

Rnd 52: Ch2, bpdc1, honeycomb Small motif 2, bpdc1, honeycomb Small motif 2, sl st in first bpdc. (48)

Rnd 53: Ch2, bpdc1, honeycomb Small motif 3, bpdc1, honeycomb Small motif 3, sl st in first bpdc. (48)

Rnd 54: Ch2, bpdc1, honeycomb Small motif 4, bpdc1, honeycomb Small motif 4, sl st in first bpdc. (48)

Rnd 55: Ch2, bpdc1, honeycomb Small motif 5, bpdc1, honeycomb Small motif 5, sl st in first bpdc. (48)

Rnd 56: Ch2, bpdc1, honeycomb Small motif 6, bpdc1, honeycomb Small motif 6, sl st in first bpdc. (48)

Rnd 57: Ch2, fpdc1 in each stitch around, sl st in first fpdc. (48)

Rnds 58-64: Ch2, *fpdc1, bpdc1*, repeat * to * around, sl st in first fpdc. (48)

Fasten off and weave in ends.

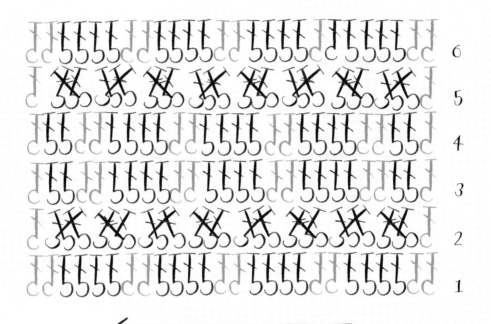

6
5
4
3
2
1

**SIZE: MEDIUM**

**HONEYCOMB MEDIUM MOTIF 1:** Bpdc2, *fpdc4, bpdc2*, repeat * to * 3 more times.

**HONEYCOMB MEDIUM MOTIF 2:** Bpdc1, *skip 1 stitch, fpdc2, make 1 fptrc in the stitch you just skipped but behind the 2 previous fpdc, skip 2 stitches, fptrc1, make 1 fpdc in each of the 2 stitches you just skipped but in front of the previous fptrc*, repeat from * to * 3 more times, bpdc1.

**HONEYCOMB MEDIUM MOTIF 3-4:** Bpdc1, fpdc2, bpdc2, fpdc4, bpdc2, fpdc4, bpdc2, fpdc4, bpdc2, fpdc2, bpdc1.

**HONEYCOMB MEDIUM MOTIF 5:** Bpdc1, *skip 2 stitches, fptrc1, make 1 fpdc in each of the 2 stitches you just skipped but in front of the previous fptrc, skip 1 stitch, fpdc2, make 1 fptrc in the stitch you just skipped but behind the 2 previous fpdc*, repeat from * to * 3 more times, bpdc1.

**HONEYCOMB MEDIUM MOTIF 6:** Just like Honeycomb Medium motif 1.

Rnd 1:  Start with a magic loop, ch2 (first ch2 doesn't count as first dc throughout the pattern), 6dc in the loop, sl st in first dc. (6)

Rnd 2:  Ch2, 2fpdc in each stitch around, sl st in first fpdc. (12)

Rnd 3:  Ch2, *fpdc1, 2fpdc in next st*, repeat * to * 2 more times, hdc1, 2fpdc in next st, repeat * to * 2 more times, sl st in first fpdc. (18)

Rnd 4:  Ch2, *fpdc2, 2fpdc in next st*, repeat * to * 2 more times, hdc1, fpdc1, 2fpdc in next st, repeat * to * 2 more times, sl st in first fpdc. (24)

Rnd 5:  Ch2, *fpdc3, 2fpdc in next st*, repeat * to * 2 more times, hdc1, fpdc2, 2fpdc in next st, repeat * to * 2 more times, sl st in first fpdc. (30)

Rnd 6:  Ch2, *fpdc4, 2fpdc in next st*, repeat * to * 2 more times, hdc1, fpdc3, 2fpdc in next st, repeat * to * 2 more times, sl st in first fpdc. (36)

Rnd 7:  Ch2, *fpdc5, 2fpdc in next st*, repeat * to * 2 more times, hdc1, fpdc4, 2fpdc in next st, repeat * to * 2 more times, sl st in first fpdc. (42)

Rnd 8: Ch2, *fpdc6, 2fpdc in next st*, repeat * to * 2 more times, hdc1, fpdc5, 2fpdc in next st, repeat * to * 2 more times, sl st in first fpdc. (48)

Rnd 9: Ch2, *fpdc7, 2fpdc in next st*, repeat * to * 2 more times, hdc1, fpdc6, 2fpdc in next st, repeat * to * 2 more times, sl st in first fpdc. (54)

Rnd 10: Ch2, fpdc27, hdc1, honeycomb Medium motif 1, sl st in first fpdc. (54)

Rnd 11: Ch2, fpdc27, hdc1, honeycomb Medium motif 2, sl st in first fpdc. (54)

Rnds 12-13: Ch2, fpdc27, hdc1, honeycomb Medium motif 3-4, sl st in first fpdc. (54)

Rnd 14: Ch2, fpdc27, hdc1, honeycomb Medium motif 5, sl st in first fpdc. (54)

Rnd 15: Ch2, fpdc27, hdc1, honeycomb Medium motif 6, sl st in first fpdc. (54)

Rnds 16-37: Repeat Rnds 10-15; you'll end with Rnd 13.

Rnd 38: Ch2, 2fpdc in next st, fpdc25, 2fpdc in next st, hdc1, honeycomb Medium motif 5, sl st in first fpdc. (56)

Rnd 39: Ch2, fpdc1, 2fpdc in next st, fpdc25, 2fpdc in next st, fpdc1, hdc1, honeycomb Medium motif 6, sl st in first fpdc. (58)

Rnd 40: Ch2, fpdc2, 2fpdc in next st, fpdc25, 2fpdc in next st, fpdc2, hdc1, honeycomb Medium motif 1, sl st in first fpdc. (60)

Rnd 41: Ch2, fpdc3, 2fpdc in next st, fpdc25, 2fpdc in next st, fpdc3, hdc1, honeycomb Medium motif 2, sl st in first fpdc. (62)

Rnd 42: Ch2, fpdc4, 2fpdc in next st, fpdc25, 2fpdc in next st, fpdc4, hdc1, honeycomb Medium motif 3, sl st in first fpdc. (64)

Rnd 43: Ch2, fpdc5, 2fpdc in next st, fpdc25, 2fpdc in next st, fpdc5, hdc1, honeycomb Medium motif 4, sl st in first fpdc. (66)

Rnd 44: Ch2, fpdc6, 2fpdc in next st, fpdc25, 2fpdc in next st, fpdc6, hdc1, honeycomb Medium motif 5, sl st in first fpdc. (68)

Rnd 45: Ch2, fpdc7, 2fpdc in next st, fpdc25, 2fpdc in next st, fpdc7, hdc1, honeycomb Medium motif 6, sl st in first fpdc. (70)

Rnd 46: Ch2, fpdc7, fpdc2tog, fpdc25, fpdc2tog, fpdc7, hdc1, honeycomb Medium motif 1, sl st in first fpdc. (68)

Rnd 47: Ch2, fpdc6, fpdc2tog, fpdc25, fpdc2tog, fpdc6, hdc1, honeycomb Medium motif 2, sl st in first fpdc. (66)

Rnd 48: Ch2, fpdc5, fpdc2tog, fpdc25, fpdc2tog, fpdc5, hdc1, honeycomb Medium motif 3, sl st in first fpdc. (64)

Rnd 49: Ch2, fpdc4, fpdc2tog, fpdc25, fpdc2tog, fpdc4, hdc1, honeycomb Medium motif 4, sl st in first fpdc. (62)

Rnd 50: Ch2, fpdc3, fpdc2tog, fpdc25, fpdc2tog, fpdc3, hdc1, honeycomb Medium motif 5, sl st in first fpdc. (60)

Rnd 51: Ch2, fpdc2, fpdc2tog, fpdc25, fpdc2tog, fpdc2, hdc1, honeycomb Medium motif 6, sl st in first fpdc. (58)

Rnd 52: Ch2, fpdc1, fpdc2tog, fpdc25, fpdc2tog, fpdc1, hdc1, honeycomb Medium motif 1, sl st in first fpdc. (56)

Rnd 53: Ch2, fpdc2tog, fpdc25, fpdc2tog, hdc1, honeycomb Medium motif 2, sl st in first fpdc. (54)

Rnd 54: Ch2, bpdc1, honeycomb Medium motif 3, bpdc1, honeycomb Medium motif 3, sl st in first bpdc. (54)

Rnd 55: Ch2, bpdc1, honeycomb Medium motif 4, bpdc1, honeycomb Medium motif 4, sl st in first bpdc. (54)

Rnd 56: Ch2, bpdc1, honeycomb Medium motif 5, bpdc1, honeycomb Medium motif 5, sl st in first bpdc. (54)

Rnd 57: Ch2, bpdc1, honeycomb Medium motif 6, bpdc1, honeycomb Medium motif 6, sl st in first bpdc. (54)

Rnd 58: Ch2, bpdc1, honeycomb Medium motif 1, bpdc1, honeycomb Medium motif 1, sl st in first bpdc. (54)

Rnd 59: Ch2, bpdc1, honeycomb Medium motif 2, bpdc1, honeycomb Medium motif 2, sl st in first bpdc. (54)

Rnds 60-65: Repeat Rnds 54-59.

Rnd 66: Ch2, bpdc1, honeycomb Medium motif 3, bpdc1, honeycomb Medium motif 3, sl st in first bpdc. (54)

Rnd 67: Ch2, fpdc1 in each stitch around, sl st in first fpdc. (54)

Rnds 68-74: Ch2, *fpdc1, bpdc1*, repeat * to * around, sl st in first fpdc. (54)

Fasten off and weave in ends.

# Chapter 6

## tips & extras

------------------------------

### Add Labels

A very nice way to personalize your socks is adding a label! Many vendors for personalized tags can be found online.

### Make an Anti-slip Coating

These wonderfully soft slippers can of course slip a bit on a smooth floor. You can prevent this by applying a non-slip agent to the bottoms. A few to try are Sock-stop from Rico design, Stop & Go from Lana Grossa or Abs-Latex from Regia.

### Add a Handmade Wrapper

Crocheted socks are of course perfect to give as a present, and it's even nicer if you style them with a homemade wrapper. Add details such as the name of the giver and maker or size and how to properly wash them (you can find this on the label of your yarn).

### Make a Scarf

Depending on the size socks you have made, you often have left-over yarn. These leftovers you can of course make into more socks, but you can also do endless other projects. For example, think of a scrappy blanket or a scarf. In the photo at left, you'll see I've made the leftovers from the socks in this book into a beautiful Windmill Scarf (pattern available from my Ravelry or my Etsy store AlaSascha). Try any number of colorful patterns to use up your yarn ends.

# ACKNOWLEDGMENTS

My husband **Josse**, daughters **Mijntje** and **Julia**, and son **Olivier**, thanks for your support and of course for borrowing your legs and feet for the pictures!

My mother, father, parents-in-law, brother, sisters-in-law, brothers-in-law, family, friends, colleagues: Thank you all!

**Ans Baart**, this book wouldn't be here without you! From the idea to the support and even elaboration of the many socks, thanks!

**Dennis de Gussem**, thank you very much for joining us and testing.

Also a huge thank-you to all testers who have tried these patterns with so much love and dedication! **Bianca van der Maarel**, **Chantal Put-Schoutene**, **Colette Hendriks**, **Corina van Krieken**, **Diane van Lier-Noordenbos**, **Emanuelle Overeem**, **Eveline Koeleman**, **Joke Stuurman**, **Karin Frenzen**, **Tine Oetzman**, **Lisa van de Graaf-Slootman**, **Monique Schut**, **Sofie De Zutter**. And my English-language testers **Annie Shelton**, **Morea Petersen**, **Debbie Allen Richardson**, **Susan Higbe**, **Yee Wong**, **Christina Dunlap**, **Mandy Jo**, **Emily Truman**, and **Leslie Mansfield**.

Thank you, **Debby Groeneveld**, for your help and support on the Facebook groups, and also **Peggy Jansen-Peters**, thank you for your support and contribution!

**Esther Befort**, thank you for the beautiful pictures again, support, and creativity!

Publisher **Kosmos** and all dear employees, thank you for making this book possible. I love that you have been loyal to me for so many years, giving the opportunity and confidence to continue publishing books.

**Stackpole Books** and **Candi Derr**, thank you so much for giving me the opportunity to have my books translated and published abroad. I feel so honored with this amazing privilege.

**Julia Foldenyi** and **Irina Fomichev** from Shared Stories I'd love to thank you for helping to make this translation possible. Thank you for all of your hard work!

**Jessica Kouwenhoven**, thank you for the beautiful crochet hooks that you made for me! **Allan Marshal**, thank you so much for the beautiful crochet hooks you've made for me! **Phaedra Tanghe**, thank you for the beautiful handmade stitch markers! **Liza Joof**, thank you very much for the great bags! **Caroline Wetenkamp**, thank you very much for the beautiful shoes! **Jeanet Jaffari-Schroevers**, thanks for the beautiful yarns, your support and contribution! **Kristel Neuckens**, thank you for your support and trust! And thank you, **Bert Noorderijk**, for your support and involvement!

In addition, there are a lot of companies and their employees who have collaborated on the materials for this book. Thank you very much for that!

# SPONSORS

**Yarns**
G Brouwer en Zn Fournituren Groothandel
De Bondt B. V. Groothandel in Fournituren
Lana Grossa
BN Agenturen
Borgo de Pazzi
Blij dat ik brei (Glad to Knit)

**Handmade Crochet Hooks**
Jessica Kouwenhoven (@studioforestfriends)
https://forest-friends.wixsite.com/blog
Bowltech Crochet Hooks ergonomic
https://www.facebook.com/allanmarshall393/

**Handmade Stitch Markers**
Phaedra Tanghe
https://www.facebook.com/byphaedra/
**Bag p. 51**
JOOF Tassen
www.shopjoof.com

**Shoes**
Cwears
www.cwears.nl

## ABOUT THE AUTHOR

**Sascha Blase-Van Wagtendonk**, known for her crochet ragdoll patterns and crochet blog A La Sascha (www.alasascha.com), publishes a variety of crochet patterns in both Dutch and English. She is the author of Crochet Ragdolls and several crochet books in Dutch.